RULE
THE
WORLD

Master the power of
storytelling to inspire,
influence and succeed

Paul Furlong

Fisher King Publishing

RULE THE WORLD

Fisher King Publishing
The Old Barn
York Road
Thirsk
YO7 3AD
England
fisherkingpublishing.co.uk

For Amy, Alina and Elise
as we write our story together

Contents

Introduction

"Those that tell the stories rule the world."

– Plato, Greek philosopher

It's just before 3am in New York on the 9th November 2016. Donald Trump, with his whole family in tow, is walking down the stairs onto the stage in a balloon-festooned ballroom at the Hilton Hotel to deliver his presidential acceptance speech to the rousing theme from the Harrison Ford movie Air Force One. Cheers of "U-S-A, U-S-A!" emanate from the ecstatic crowd. 'Make America Great Again' hats are everywhere. There's even one encased in a glass box on the stage. Vice-President-Elect Mike Pence and his family are already on the stage having introduced the incoming president. The air of expectation and excitement in the room is palpable.

Meanwhile, across town, the mood couldn't be more different. Hilary Clinton and her team sit in shock as her campaign manager John Podesta makes a brief appearance to send her supporters home from the Javits Center ballroom under the massive glass ceiling so many had thought she was going to shatter.

How could this have happened? Everything that everyone said couldn't happen had just happened. The man that every political commentator had written off from the very beginning, that every commentator said wouldn't make it past the primaries, and certainly would never beat Hillary Clinton, had just clinched the presidency of the United States of America – the most powerful job in the world.

Looking at it from the other side, how did Hillary Clinton,

possibly one of the most qualified people in history for the job of President of the United States – Yale graduate, attorney, first lady, senator, secretary of state – lose the election? Political scholars will debate this for decades and possibly even centuries to come.

My answer is fairly straightforward and probably oversimplified, but I'll give it to you anyway.

Hilary focused on telling people about what they needed using facts and figures, and politics. In essence, she told them what to think. In contrast, Trump told them how to feel by telling stories. He inspired people. He instilled emotions through his storytelling. Because, what Trump knew was that the difference between emotion, elicited through storytelling, and reason, elicited through facts and figures, is that reason leads to conclusions and emotion leads to action.

For me, the most important story Trump ever shared was told in just four words – 'Make America Great Again'. So simple, yet so complex in its making. As we go through all the principles of storytelling in this book, see how many of them Trump and his team managed to include in these four words. It's staggering.

And that's the key difference. It doesn't matter if you're selling a product, a service or an idea, and it doesn't matter whether you are sat in a sales meeting, delivering a presentation, or developing copy for your website or social media. If you simply throw facts and figures and graphs and statistics at people, you will not connect with them and you're unlikely to convince them to buy in to what you're selling. The thing that is going to connect people to you and get them to take the action that you want them to is a good, well-told story.

This book is written for anyone looking to improve their life, grow their business, or make a difference in the world. A well-timed, well-told story will help you to do this because it will guide you to inspire, lead, and generate results.

Dip into any chapter in this book and you will be able to immediately apply what you've read to your storytelling and see an instant improvement in both your ability and outcomes. It is, however, written in a particular order so that the principles laid out at the start of the book lay a foundation for the principles that come later.

As you go, you'll notice my love of movies and great TV shows. Whenever I look for an allegory or metaphor, rather than turn to Aesop or William Shakespeare, my mind naturally goes to the movies that I have connected with the most in my life – The Lord of the Rings, The Godfather, The Matrix, and some of the most quotable films and TV shows that, whether my wife has seen them or not, she can now recite in her sleep thanks to how often I reference them – the likes of Anchorman, Scrubs and The Big Lebowski.

You will also find at the end of every chapter some success tasks for you to implement. Please take them seriously and make the time to carry them out. Some will take only two minutes, some a tad longer, but by implementing them I guarantee that you will be able to embed the principles discussed in this book more quickly and thoroughly into your everyday storytelling habits and see even better results.

Your first success task is to think of a story that you tell regularly in your day to day work life. It might be in a sales situation, it may be a case study, or it could be a presentation you deliver on stage or to your teams. We're going to work on that story as we go through the book. Have you got it in your mind? Great.

So then, if you're sitting comfortably, I'll begin.

Chapter 1: Why Story?

"Story, as it turns out, was crucial to our evolution –
more so than opposable thumbs. Opposable thumbs
let us hang on; story told us what to hang on to."
– Lisa Cron, 'Wired for Story'

Imagine an island paradise home to the richest marine environment in the world, lush with coastal mangroves, deciduous forests and high mountainside wilderness, a panorama pockmarked with fissures and hot springs that spew steam against a backdrop of volcanic calderas.

Somewhere close to 44,000 years ago on this Indonesian island of Sulawesi, a group of people gathered in a cave to tell a story. It's a story of a fight between a blast of hunters and their prey – wild pigs and dwarf buffalo known as anoa. The hunters, however, aren't quite human – they're animal-human hybrids. Their faces are distorted: one has a beak, another a tail. And the prey that they hunt are monstrously huge, many times larger than their attackers. It's a story as old as time: good versus evil, man against beast. It's a story of a spiritual battle.

How do we know that this storytelling event took place? Because it's painted on the wall of a cave at a site called Liang Bulu'Sipong 4. It's four and a half metres long and stands three metres tall, illuminated by a shaft of light through an opening in the northeast wall of the cave.

As far as we know, this is the oldest story ever recorded.

Throughout the history of the human race, storytelling has been the foremost method of passing information on. This began when we started to control fire as hunter-gatherers about one million years ago, which allowed us to extend the day and gave time for social activities and the sharing of stories. These stories stirred the imagination, helped people recollect and understand others in nearby tribes, healed misunderstandings within the group, and communicated information about how the tribe expected their members to behave as a small-scale society.

As we became more sophisticated, stories continued to be the main source of collecting and communicating information. In every culture throughout history, there are records of oral and written traditions of storytelling, like the Bible, the Odyssey and the epics of India. These stories were so essential to specific cultures that they were learned and passed down orally through many generations prior to being written.

In West African culture, there is a similar oral tradition. A griot is charged with keeping the stories of the village. Everyone in the village tells the griot their stories, and it is the griot's job to remember them all so that they can pass on the stories to future generations. When the griot gets old, they tell all the stories to someone else. They say in West Africa that when a griot dies, it's like a library has burnt down. The tradition continues to this day.

The most amazing thing is this; anthropologists still can't agree when complex language developed, but it is thought to have been formed towards the end of the Palaeolithic era around the time that the cave paintings in Indonesia were created and long after we as a species controlled fire. So even before and while language as we know it today was evolving, stories have been our primary way of collecting and communicating information.

Simply put, humans are wired to tell stories.

So if we're wired to tell stories, how and why is this the case?

Firstly, our brains love patterns. Look around where you're sitting. Can you see any patterns? Did your brain automatically assign meaning to the pattern even though inherently there isn't one there? That's natural. Your brain loves to do that. It loves to find patterns in arbitrary things – faces, letters, musical notes – and then make up a meaning about them, knowing a particular collection of eyes, nose and mouth is the face of your dad, that a certain collection of letters makes up a particular word, or that specific notes make up a recognisable song.

Stories are recognisable patterns that the brain tries to assign meaning to. We hear them and try to make them personal to ourselves. Even when there's no story there, we try to make them up.

In a 1944 experiment in Massachusetts, students were shown a film of two triangles and a circle moving on the screen and asked to describe what was going on. Out of thirty-four students, thirty-three described the scene with humanesque narratives, suggesting that the circle looked "worried", that the big triangle felt "rage and frustration", and that the woman (circle) was trying to escape as the two men (triangles) fought.

This is described as pareidolia – the imagined perception of a pattern or meaning where it does not actually exist, such as seeing shapes in clouds, seeing faces in inanimate objects or abstract patterns, or hearing hidden messages in music.

We're constantly seeking out stories and will get our fix wherever we can.

Todd Handy, a cognitive science professor in the Department

of Psychology at the University of British Columbia, said this obsession with stories is what makes humans different from all other species, even our nearest animal relatives.

"Human brains evolved to be good at storytelling," Handy said, "and the neuroscience behind storytelling is what makes it so effective. Storytelling fits with what our brains evolved to do, which is to remember our past experiences. Our memories are stories of what we've experienced previously, and we have stories of what we anticipate for the future."

Being able to remember the past to learn from our mistakes and daydream to imagine the future is necessary for adapting and surviving.

The stories that our ancestors listened to, or that we now read, listen to and watch, become nearly as good as the lived experience and are therefore implanted in our minds. That's why we can effortlessly recall plots of novels, quotes from movies, and slogans from ads.

"Storytelling taps into the same neural systems we use for recalling the past and imagining the future, that's probably why it's such an effective mnemonic for us," Handy said, "Our brains are geared towards remembering stories."

The other element of memory that is key to storytelling is our collective memory. Collective memory is the shared pool of memories, knowledge and information that we have as a society. So when we deliver a well-told story, we tap into the memories, knowledge and information of our listeners and allow them to fill in the gaps around what we don't say so that their subconscious does most of the work for them. We just need to know which buttons to press and how to press them.

Have you seen *Inception*? In the film, Leonardo DiCaprio's character Cobb is a thief who steals corporate secrets by entering the dreams of company employees. He is wanted by the authorities for his alleged role in his wife's murder and his only chance at redemption is to perform the impossible: an inception. Inception is the inverse of stealing information from people's minds – it is the planting of an idea.

Do you remember the scene where Cobb is talking with Elliot Page's character Ariadne at the Parisian café before the dream falls apart and the whole place starts to explode one element at a time? At the start of that scene, Cobb says to Ariadne, "You create the world of the dream, you bring the subject into the dream, and they fill it with their subconscious." This is what I'm talking about. This is the collective memory. You create the world of the story, you bring the listener into the story, and they fill it with their collective memory.

On the flip side of this, memories can be strengthened by story. I remember when I was revising for my exams in school. If there was something I couldn't remember, I'd head downstairs to ask my mum for help. She has a great method that people around the world use to help them remember things. She'd put what I had to remember into a story, and because my mum is a little off the wall, it was never a normal story. Most of the time, the things I had to remember where scientific processes, none of which my mum understood, but she had a great knack of hearing the sounds that words made and associating them with memorable images and then tying them together into a story.

Our brains pay much better attention to information when it's in the form of a story. In one study, four people were asked to memorise twelve lists of ten words. Half of the people studied the lists, rehearsed them, and tried to memorise them without the benefit of turning them into a story. On average, the members of this group remembered thirteen percent of the words. The other half created stories of their own invention from the words and remembered ninety-three percent. This goes to show that if you can associate the things that you want to remember with structures you already have in your mind, the easier it is going to be to remember. When you want to retrieve that memory, you then have multiple entry points to access it from.

Do you remember a few moments ago when we were discussing neuroscience? I want to tell you about what for me is the most miraculous and most important phenomenon that happens when we tell stories – the brain of the person listening to the story can synchronise with the brain of the person telling the story through something called 'mirror neurones'.

This discovery began, as many discoveries do, in monkeys. The scientists at the University of Parma discovered that groups of motor neurons in the brains of macaques fired not only when a monkey performed an action but also when the monkey watched another subject perform that exact same action. If monkey A saw monkey B pick up an apple from a box, the motor neurones responsible for picking up an apple in monkey A would fire. What was even more amazing was that when the monkey heard a subject perform an action in a room nearby, their corresponding group of neurones would fire too, just from hearing the action being performed.

This experiment has been taken further into the fields of storytelling and emotion.

The phenomenon known as 'neural coupling' was demonstrated by a team of scientists at Princeton University in America led by Uri Hasson. In the experiment, a woman told a story while an fMRI (functional Magnetic Resonance Imaging) scanner tracked her brain activity.

Next, they played the recorded story to a group of volunteers while they had their brains scanned. They found that the brain activity of the storyteller and the listeners mirrored each other. When the storyteller had activity in her insula cortex, an emotional brain region, the listeners did too. When her frontal cortex fired, so did theirs – they experienced the exact same brain pattern. As Dr Hasson said, "By simply telling a story, the woman could plant ideas, thoughts and emotions into the listeners' brains."

But it's not just about the physical reactions; it's also about emotions and empathy. In an experiment at the Netherlands Institute for Neuroscience in Amsterdam, Christian Keysers and Valeria Gazzola observed that seeing or hearing about another person's action or pain can trigger portions of the same neural pathways responsible for carrying out those actions and experiencing those feelings and emotions directly.

Keysers said, "When we witness what happens to others, [we] activate our own emotions and sensations as if we felt the same." In his book 'Mirroring People: The Science of Empathy and How We Connect with Others', Marco Iacoboni asks, "Why do we give ourselves over to emotion during the carefully crafted, heartrending scenes in certain movies? Because mirror neurons in our brains recreate for us the distress we see on the screen."

It's not just our neurones that respond to stories. Studies show our endocrine system activates too. Hormones released include dopamine, oxytocin and endorphins. These could all be broadly categorised as 'feel good' hormones, meaning we feel much more connected and endeared to someone telling a story and they can motivate cooperation by enhancing the sense of empathy toward the storyteller.

Oxytocin, the 'moral molecule' or love hormone, is key amongst these. Oxytocin is secreted when someone shows us kindness or when we begin to trust them, and it stimulates cooperation in others. It does this by increasing the feeling of empathy and our capacity to experience other people's emotions. In studies at Claremont Graduate University, neuroeconomist Paul J Zak and his team discovered that when people listen to a well-told story, the body releases oxytocin by the bucketful (the scientific term).

Further into the *Inception* scene I mentioned earlier, Cobb describes the process of inception to Ariadne as "shared dreaming" but, in the film, the person being incepted must be asleep. In storytelling, we can 'incept' people when they are still awake through helping them remember what we tell them, by neural coupling, and by 'hacking' their oxytocin system. We can plant ideas to influence people to our way of thinking without the dream-sharing technology that was required in the film. And thankfully, when we do it, we're not doing it for nefarious purposes. We're doing it to help people, to help them to have the life they dream of.

This is what great leaders of the past knew – that great storytelling is what sells an idea to someone, and it becomes infectious.

Think about Abraham Lincoln and his 272 word Gettysburg Address:

"Four score and seven years ago our fathers brought forth on this continent, a new nation, conceived in Liberty, and dedicated to the proposition that all men are created equal."

By telling the story that freedom was not just for idealists but that it could be fought for by each individual on the battlefield and defended by a unified nation devoted to its conservation, Lincoln transformed America. He inspired the North to persevere in their fight and forever changed how Americans viewed their nation.

How about Martin Luther King Jr's 'I Have a Dream' speech?

The story he delivered with such powerful oratory in 1963 in front of the Lincoln Memorial in Washington has inspired millions upon millions of people. Over 250,000 listeners gathered in the heat and waited for most of the day for him to come out to the lectern. The immediate impact of the speech was to put huge pressure on President Lyndon B Johnson's administration to push the civil rights laws through Congress. In 1964, the Civil Rights Act was passed, and later the following year the Voting Rights Act followed. Of course, he inspired people on the other side of the issue too, and tragically was assassinated in 1968. But his inspirational words live on over fifty-odd years later having influenced many millions of people, including the likes of Barack Obama.

When I've asked other storytellers who is the greatest storyteller of all time, the answer I get back most often is Jesus. When I ask why, I usually get the same answer; because we're over two thousand years on and his stories are still inspiring people around the world. In fact, according to Pew Research Centre, there are over two-point-four billion Christians in the world today.

Think about it. Simple stories like the Good Samaritan, the

Prodigal Son and the Lost Sheep still stand the test of time after more than two thousand years and continue to inspire billions of people. That is quite something.

So, that's a quick precis of the history and science of storytelling. I imagine that you were already bought into the concept that it's a good idea to use storytelling in your organisation to sell your products, services or ideas, but if not, I hope that I have demonstrated why storytelling is so powerful.

Success Tasks

- Search Google for the Liang Bulu'Sipong 4 cave painting.
- Look for a random pattern in your home or office. Make up a story about what's happening in the pattern.
- Below is a list of ten random words. Make up a story mnemonic to remember them all.

Juror	Snack
Trifle	Wife
Plane	Lawnmower
Juggler	Egg
Flame	Swarm

- Read the Gettysburg Address, Martin Luther King Jr's 'I Have a Dream' speech or the parable of the Prodigal Son (it can be found in the Bible in the

Book of Luke, Chapter 15, Verses 11-32).

- Watch *Inception*.

The
Setup

Chapter 2: Who's Your Audience?

"When you speak to everyone you speak to no one."
– Meredith Hill, Founder and CEO, Global Institute
for Travel Entrepreneurs (GIFTE)

A few years back, I was passed a referral from a good friend of mine into what I thought was a small local energy company. I was told they helped SMEs to reduce their energy bills. I spoke to a lovely lady there and we arranged for me to go in and spend some time with her to discover how we could potentially help the company with some video content.

When I arrived at their offices, they seemed a little bigger than I had expected, but not enough to raise too many suspicions. I was greeted by a member of the admin team who showed me to the reception area, brought me a glass of water, and we made small talk. After a couple of minutes, the lady I had spoken to on the phone came out to the reception area and dropped the bombshell that she hadn't been one hundred percent honest with me on the phone. She did represent a local energy company who helped SMEs reduce their energy bills, but the energy company was owned by the world's second largest manufacturer of LED lightbulbs and the board was in town, over from Hong Kong, and wanted to meet with me. In fact, they were in the boardroom right now, ready for me.

There's nothing like the feeling of being ambushed like that. All the preparation I had done for the meeting with the small energy company was now out of the window and all my intuition and training had to come to the forefront as I was summoned into the boardroom.

I was introduced to the fourteen or fifteen members of the board, and to the chair of the board, Jonnie, a very charming, friendly gentleman who wore jeans, a T-shirt and jacket, had long slicked-back black hair and couldn't have been older than forty-five. When he spoke, everybody listened. Jonnie asked for my credentials, which I duly gave, and told me they wanted an animation to sell their lightbulbs.

The board excitedly went through what they wanted the characters to look like, how they wanted them to move, what colour scheme they wanted, how they wanted it to sound – they had it all planned out and they were loving it. This discussion went on for about ten to fifteen minutes, but in my mind, there were a few unanswered questions, a few steps that had been missed out in their bid to jump straight to animation as the solution. So, knowing that when Jonnie spoke everybody else listened, I mustered up all my courage and interrupted.

"Excuse me, Jonnie," I said. The room fell deadly silent and everybody stared at me. Jonnie looked at me and smiled.

"First of all, no one ever interrupts me. I like it. You've got the job." I smiled and thanked Jonnie.

"I'm not quite sure I want the job yet. I think we've missed a few steps out to get to your need for an animation." You could hear a pin drop as the rest of the board waited to see what Jonnie would do.

He just laughed and said, "I like you. Now that you've interrupted, why don't you tell us more."

I explained that I was delighted that they were taking video so seriously as a way of selling their product, but that we needed to take a few steps back to work out who their target audience was. Once we knew that, we could work out what we wanted their target audience to do, and once we knew that, we could work out what story we needed to encourage them to do the thing we wanted them to do. Only then would we know which medium to use to tell the story.

So I asked them who their target audience was. For the next fifteen minutes, the members of the board discussed who their target audience was, with each board member selecting a different audience. I interjected again because it was clear that there was no consensus. My proposal to them was that I would come back three days later once they had had a chance to digest some questions to help determine who their ideal target audience was. Then we could work out what we wanted them to do, and therefore what story we should tell them and how to tell it.

This is what we did upon my return three days later. It turned out that their target audience were gruff, male, forty-five to fifty-five year old financially motivated company owners, who probably drove Mercedes or BMW-type cars, who were looking to save money on their energy bills in the big warehouses that they owned or rented. So I asked them, did they think that these gruff middle-aged men would respond well to little cartoon lightbulbs prancing around with high-pitched voices like they had originally proposed? Unanimously they agreed this was not a good idea.

In the end, what was agreed was to create short customer testimonial films of other gruff, male, forty-five to fifty-five year old financially motivated company owners, who probably drove Mercedes or BMW-type cars, talking to camera about how by using their company's LED lightbulbs they had saved a ton of money. This was the right decision (even though an animation would have been a bigger deal for me and my company) because it was the right story to tell in the right way targeted at the right audience.

Knowing your audience is absolutely key when planning your story, otherwise you may as well be telling it to the wind.

But how do we begin to define our audience so that we can refine our story to their needs?

Well, to begin with, it's just that. What do they need? And what do they want?

It's important to understand what your listener wants and needs because it informs your story. If you don't know what they want, it's hard to take them somewhere on a journey, and that's what stories are all about.

Pick your favourite movie, or any movie for that matter. Within the first ten minutes of meeting the protagonist, they'll tell you what they want. In a Disney movie, they'll probably sing it at you. Let's see. In *The Lion King*, Simba sings, "I just can't wait to be king." In Moana, Moana sings, "One day I'll know how far I'll go." And in The Hunchback of Notre Dame, Quasimodo sings, "Give me one day out there." In other movies, too, the want of the protagonist is revealed early on, though usually without singing. In *Jurassic Park*, Dr Grant wants to study palaeontology in peace. *Jane Eyre* wants to be loved. And in *Toy Story*, Woody wants to be Andy's favourite toy.

Notice that these are all external things, trying to solve inner issues with relatively surface-level solutions. That's where their needs come into play and where conflict tends to be formed in storytelling, where you can start to play with your audience a little bit by understanding what they want and playing it off against what they need.

Depending on the story, solving this need won't change anything about the character's external world, but it will always change their view of themselves and how they see the world, enabling them to better cope with any remaining external issues.

Most of the time, the thing that the character needs will be more important than the thing the character wants. Look at the list of wants above and compare them to the character's needs. Simba's need to take responsibility and live up to his father's legacy. Moana's need to find courage and lead her ancestors. Quasimodo's need to be loved. Dr Grant's need to protect the living present over the extinct past. Jane Eyre's need to find spiritual freedom. Woody's need to share Andy's love.

The character will reach a point where they become willing to sacrifice the thing that they want for the thing that they need. More often than not, this brings together the internal and external goals at the climax of the story and the character achieves both their wants and their needs.

You can now see why it is so important to understand your audience's wants and needs. When you know what they want and need, you can tell a story where your characters have the same wants and needs, and you can pit them against each other to help your audience buy in even further to what you have to offer.

The next thing we need to know about your audience is how they like to be communicated with. There are two models that we'll take a quick look at, with many books written on both subjects, so this will be a brief overview. It will help us to understand that all audience members are different and like to be communicated with on an individual basis. If we get this wrong, we may as well be speaking a foreign language to them.

We'll first look at VARK then take a whistle-stop tour of DISC.

Every one of your audience members would like to be communicated with slightly differently. One of the most accepted understandings of communication styles is VARK – Visual, Auditory, Reading/Writing and Kinaesthetic.

Someone with a preference for visual communication thinks in images, so they are partial to seeing and observing things like pictures, diagrams, written directions and more. When telling stories to this audience, try and use visuals if possible. If that's not possible, use visual language – words such as clarity, dream, illustrate and picture.

Auditory communicators tend to learn better when the subject matter is reinforced by what they can hear, because they think in terms of sound. They would much rather listen to a lecture or an audiobook than read written notes, and they often use their own voice to reinforce new concepts and ideas. You've already got this covered with an auditory story, but to make sure it's covered in other story media, use auditory words like articulate, earshot, rumour and utter.

Kinaesthetic communicators represent thoughts as feelings so they learn through experiencing or doing things. They like to get involved by acting out events or using their hands to touch and handle in order to understand concepts. When telling your story, if possible, allow your audience to interact with you or through the movement and rhythm of their body. If this isn't possible, be sure to use kinaesthetic words such as active, emotional, intuition and pressure.

Reading/writing communicators prefer to learn through written words. So, if they're reading your story, they're well covered. To make sure you're effectively communicating to them in non-written stories, ask them to take notes or recite your story back to you.

But how do you discover your audience's preferred communication style? By asking questions and listening.

A visual communicator will use phrases like, "I get the picture", "let's try to put this into perspective", "show me" and "let's have a look at that". An auditory communicator will prefer phrases like, "I hear what you are saying", "sounds good to me", "tell me" and "let's talk it through". Whereas a kinaesthetic communicator will prefer to use phrases such as, "we are getting to grips with the problem", "things are moving along smoothly", "let me try" or "how do you feel?". Reading/writing communicators will be more difficult to spot. They will be a mixture of the above.

Of course, if you are talking to a larger audience or your story is written down, then you need to mix the language up so that you use all four communication types to talk to all your audience members in their preferred style.

By understanding the kind of communicator you are yourself, you will gain a better perspective on how to implement these learning styles into your storytelling. There are many simple online questionnaires that will help you with this. A quick Google search will give you a range of choices – simply search 'VARK questionnaire' and pick one that you like the look of.

DISC is a model that separates people into four primary behavioural and communication styles: D (dominant), I (influencer), S (steady relator) and C (conscientious). Generally, people have a blend of all four styles but display one or two predominant behaviours.

People who fit in the dominant bracket can be blunt, competitive, anger quickly, and are able to see the big picture, so when communicating with people in this bracket, get to the point.

Those who fit easily into the influencing quadrant are optimistic, enthusiastic, love to collaborate, are trusting, and don't like to be ignored, so when communicating with influencers, focus on people and feelings.

Steady people are very loyal, humble and supportive. They don't like to be rushed, so when communicating with them, approach them in a calm manner.

The conscientious cohort are process-driven; they love objective reasoning, and because of the time they put into this, they don't like to be wrong. When communicating with them, be detail-oriented.

Again, if you're telling your story to just one person, it's fairly easy to get your communication style right. Go in as a steady communicator (it's the least offensive) and watch how they respond. If they ask for more detail, then you'll know that they fit comfortably in the conscientious bracket. If they start to show frustration at the level of detail you're including in your story, then you'll know they're likely to be a D and you need to pivot your storytelling and communication style to that of a dominant communicator.

However, if your story is to a room full of people or it's a written story, it becomes more of a challenge. You have to satisfy all four of the styles. You have to include enough detail to satisfy a C without having too much detail to frustrate a D. You need to have enough enthusiasm to connect with an I whilst also being calm enough to placate an S. It's a tricky business. With practise, you'll get there, and we will come back to this in later chapters.

In the meantime, as with VARK, by understanding your own DISC profile you will gain a better perspective on how to implement it into your storytelling. There are many DISC questionnaires online that will help you with this. Look on Google or use online software such as Crystal Knows that will help you predict a prospect's communication style by analysing text samples, assessment responses, and other attributes of theirs from the likes of their LinkedIn profile and website.

The other thing that you may want to know about your audience in advance of delivering your story to them is what demographic, psychographic, behavioural and geographic brackets they might fit into.

Demographics is the study of a population based on factors such as age, race and sex. Psychographics is used to describe traits of humans based on psychological attributes. Psychographics include personality, values, opinions, attitudes, interests and lifestyles. Behavioural segmentation is based on how the customer acts including purchasing habits, brand interactions and user status. Geographics is where somebody is based.

Think back to the story that I told at the start of this chapter about gruff, male, forty-five to fifty-five year old financially motivated company owners, who probably drive Mercedes or BMW-type cars, who were looking to save money on their energy bills in the big warehouses that they owned or rented. Knowing their demographics, psychographics, behaviours and geographics helped to tell the right story. An animation may have been better suited to children aged two to seven who were motivated by make-believe play with lots of stuffed toys, looking for their parents to buy more so they could play tea parties. Now I've just taken that to the extreme. Animated marketing content can be used for many great campaigns, particularly for explaining complex products and services in a simple and emotionally engaging way to the right demographic, but it wouldn't have been right in the lightbulb context. It's so important to understand you audience from all angles. I think the horrible business jargon for this is the '360-view'.

But how do you know all these things about your audience? How do you know their wants and needs? How do you know their communication styles or their psychographics and demographics?

You need to do your research. This may be as simple as asking them if you're sat opposite in a one-on-one situation. If you have time beforehand, do some due-diligence – ask someone who knows them or look them up online. If you're delivering a talk, research your audience by asking the event organiser who will be in the room. If you're writing your story, research your publication's readership so you know who will be reading it.

The great thing with any live audience is that you get real-time feedback. You can see, hear and feel how your audience is reacting to your story. If they're responding well to how you're telling your story, carry on. Why change a winning formula? But if you're getting a hostile response or no response at all, you may need to look at your communication style, playing off the want versus need in a different way, or rethinking your psychographic research. At the end of the day, the best storytellers know more about people than they do about the latest tactic or tool. It comes down to being able to read people, connect with people, and reach out to them using their language.

Success Tasks

- Watch your favourite film again. What is the main character's want? What is their need? How do the filmmakers play them off against each other for dramatic effect? How does this juxtaposition of want versus need resolve at the end of the film?
- Write a list of ten visual words, ten auditory words and ten kinaesthetic words.
- Take a VARK test online to understand what type of learner/communicator you are.
- Take a DISC test online to understand your profile.
- Look at your diary. When is the story that came to mind when you read the introduction next likely to be delivered? Do some research into the person or people that you will be presenting to before you come face-to-face with them. How much can you find out about them to help you prepare your story in terms of their communication styles and their demographic, psychographic, behavioural and geographic profiles?

Chapter 3: Begin with the End in Mind

"You may get to the very top of the ladder, and then find it has not been leaning against the right wall."

– Allen Raine, novelist

Do you love road trip movies? I love them. To my mind, there are two types of road trip movies. There's the type like *Little Miss Sunshine*, which tells the story of a dysfunctional family who are determined to get their young daughter Olive into the finals of the Little Miss Sunshine Beauty Pageant, but in order to get there in time, they need to take a cross-country trip in their VW bus. It's a delightful film full of quirky and relatable characters, funny and melancholic moments, and a brilliant story arc. Other films that fit into this road movie category would include *The Lord of the Rings* and *Borat: Cultural Learnings of America for Make Benefit Glorious Nation of Kazakhstan*.

The other type of road trip movie is the type like *Sideways*. It tells the story of Miles and Jack who embark on a meandering road trip through California's wine country the week before Jack's wedding. Again, it's a great film with eccentric yet everyday characters, amusing and nostalgic scenes, and a well thought out plot. Other films that fit into this road movie category would include *Almost Famous* and *The Motorcycle Diaries*.

But what's the difference between the two types of road trip movies? The first type, the *Little Miss Sunshine* type, has a clear and defined destination or goal in mind, whereas the second type, the *Sideways* type, doesn't. What this means in all the films that follow the former narrative arc is that the characters in these stories reach their destination, while the characters in the latter arc end up back where they started.

So it is with your storytelling to influence and inspire your audience.

Once you know who your audience are, you need to know what goal or outcome you want from them once you've told them your story. In Stephen R Covey's book 'The 7 Habits of Highly Effective People', he calls this "beginning with the end in mind". If you don't have a goal or outcome in mind, how will you work out how you are going to get there? How will you know if you've succeeded, failed or ended up somewhere in between if you don't know where you're aiming for? Knowing your end goal or outcome can also spur you on to success, like the characters in *Little Miss Sunshine*. Once they knew what they wanted to achieve and where they were headed, they could plan their route and encourage each other in their low moments to keep going on to the competition for the sake of Olive and her dream of winning. Knowing what you want your audience to do once they've heard your story will allow the rest of the principles in this book to act as your road map to your final destination.

We will talk in Chapter Sixteen about how to compose a compelling call to action to get your audience to buy into what you are selling, but for now it's important to know exactly the outcome you want from telling your story. There's no point in going to all the effort of planning and telling an amazing story to get to the end of it and find that the point you're trying to make is going to lead your audience to take a different action than the one you want them to.

That action you want them to take may also not be what you think it is at first thought, so really think it through.

You may think you want someone to 'buy now' when in fact you really want them to get in touch with you so that you can qualify them first to check that you want to work with them. You may think you want someone to refer you directly to someone straight away, when in fact what you really want is to sit down with the person who is going to refer you so that you can give them more information to help make the referral more successfully. You may think you want your team to work harder, but are they working harder at the right tasks or simply working harder on the wrong tasks and burning themselves out?

Now is the time to get this right, otherwise every step we make together along this journey is going to lead to the outcome you set now. If that outcome is not the right outcome, you are going to end up some distance away from where you should be and are going to have to undo a number of steps on the process ahead to get back. Before moving on, be sure that the outcome you have in mind is the right outcome.

Success Tasks

- Write down the outcomes you want from your audience after you've told them your story.

Chapter 4: How to Grab Attention

"A-I-D-A. Attention, interest, decision, action.
Attention – do I have your attention? Interest – are
you interested? I know you are because it's fuck or
walk. You close or you hit the bricks! Decision – have
you made your decision for Christ?!
And action. A-I-D-A..."

– Blake, Glengarry Glen Ross

This quote comes midway through one of the greatest monologues in movie history. Now, I'm not usually one for a monologue. I find them to be full of exposition, badly written, or badly delivered. But not here.

David Mamet added this scene to the Pulitzer Prize-winning script of his play of the same name to add length because the play is quite short by movie standards. In it we see Alec Baldwin deliver a crackling Pattonesque tirade of abuse at his unsuspecting victims. He is the motivational speaker from hell. If you've never seen the film, it's a masterpiece and well worth checking out. This scene alone is worth watching over and over again for its writing and acting, not just from Baldwin but from Ed Harris, Jack Lemon, Alan Arkin and Kevin Spacey. If your day needs a little sadistic haranguing, you'll find the scene on YouTube to watch in your own time.

The reason I bring up this scene is because of the AIDA principle that Blake raises. It's very important at the start of your story that you grab your audience's attention (holding interest, creating a decision and taking action will be talked about in later chapters). But how do we do this?

Starting on the action is a great place to begin. Think about any of the best openings to movies. The first one that sprung immediately to my mind is *The Dark Knight*, followed instantly by *Heat* (Christopher Nolan even references the scene from *Heat* in the opening to *The Dark Knight* by including William Fichtner as the bank manager in the scene).

What scenes they both are. In *The Dark Knight*, we open with that heart-pounding drum and 'bwaaam' sound that we now so readily associate with Christopher Nolan movies. We swoop across the roof tops of Gotham towards a high-rise glass building. Suddenly, one of the windows in the building shatters as a man in a clown mask shoots a grappling hook through it. A high-pitched violin that we'll come to know as the Joker's theme plays in the background, as elsewhere we push in on a clown mask in the hand of someone stood on a curb side as a car screeches around the corner and picks him up. He dons the mask.

The man who fired the grappling hook through the window now zipwires with a second man from his building to the rooftop of another. We're not sure what's happening, but something is going down. Back in the car, two masked men and the man they picked up are talking about 'the job' and how they're going to split the shares of the spoils. They sneak into the bank, fire their machine guns and start to take hostages. The action continues. I'm sure you've seen the film so there's no need for me to go on, but the action grips you straight away, as it does in *Heat*. And what a way Michael Mann starts that film – again, without going into the detail, it's straight into the action of a heist, and so meticulous too.

In your storytelling, you can do the same – get straight into the action.

"There I was, between the bear cubs and their mother..."

"I'd never been put on the spot like that before..."

"Michael, the director, looked at me and said in front of everyone that I was going to direct the episode..."

How about if you start by asking a question? Have I got your attention now? The simple act of asking a question draws people in.

Questions that generate curiosity influence our brain to want to know more and, more often than not, they want to know 'WIIFM' – what's in it for me? So long as your question is crafted in a way that leaves them leaning in to find out the answer, you've got them hooked.

By asking a question, you are inviting your listeners to participate in your story. It immediately draws your audience in, flicking a switch from passive to active participation.

However, you shouldn't start with a question that can be easily answered with 'no' because people will answer it and switch off. This is called Betteridge's law (of headlines). Betteridge's law was established in the print media industry and says that "Any headline ending in a question mark can be answered by the word no." So, when starting with a question, only use a question that defies Betteridge's law. Here are some examples of poor questions that fall right into the trap of being easily answered with no.

Can farming practices in Oklahoma solve climate change?

Can sensors scientifically prove UFOs exist?

Does bad grammar stand in the way of true love?

It's probably unlikely that farmers in Oklahoma have solved climate change, that UFOs can be proved by sensors, and that grammar and love are intrinsically linked.

However, a clever closed question where the answer is obviously no, such as "do you want your career to fail?", can be used because, despite it being very easy to answer and everyone (hopefully) would give you the same answer, your audience would be drawn in to find out what you said next.

Probing questions – those that start with who, where, what, when, how and why – are usually better placed to get people thinking and to draw them in.

Think about how they're used in newspaper headlines to grab your attention and how they are so obviously used in clickbait. The number of times I see clickbait and the question is so well phrased and, despite the fact that I know it's clickbait, I'm still tempted to click it. Thankfully, my rational brain jumps in and takes over at the last second.

Take a look at some of these newspaper and clickbait headlines to see how they draw you into the story…

Are You Making These Embarrassing Mistakes at Work?

World Bank requires autistic accountants. Can it maintain them?

What's the Secret to Keeping Your Weeds at Bay (Year After Year)?

You could also choose to be provocative at the start of your story. Look at how I started this chapter. I bet it got your attention. Yeah, using a naughty word isn't that provocative these days, but in a book where there hasn't been another naughty word used yet, it probably stood out.

You can also quote some provocative facts or statistics. Pick a TED Talk at random and I will bet it starts with a surprising statement that gets you thinking. In Jorge Soto's TED Talk, he starts by claiming, "One out of three people sitting in this audience will be diagnosed with some type of cancer." In Jane McGonigal's TED Talk, she opens by saying, "You will live seven and a half minutes longer than you would have otherwise, just because you watched this talk." And in Pamela Meyer's TED Talk, she begins with, "Ok, now I don't want to alarm anybody in this room, but it's just come to my attention that the person to your right is a liar." When you begin your story using this formula, you are creating expectations and leaving the audience wanting to know more.

The idea is to pick the most pertinent stat to connect with the audience. It's good practice to research your stats and facts, and there are plenty of websites out there. Just make sure you know your source in case someone asks you where you got your data.

And while we're on the subject of TED Talks, Ric Elias's presentation opens with the following:

"Imagine a big explosion as you climb through 3,000 feet. Imagine a plane full of smoke. Imagine an engine going clack, clack, clack." Ric is a plane crash survivor talking about his harrowing experience, and by using the word 'imagine', he leads us to use our imaginations to put ourselves in his situation.

You can do the same by starting your story using the same type of pictorial language. Prompt your audience by using commands such as "imagine", "think of" or "picture this".

Starting your story from a personal space is also a great way to grab attention. One of the stories that I share about where my love of storytelling comes from starts with the phrase, "Growing up, my brother Daniel and I would play make-believe for hours on end." This creates an emotional connection with my audience because immediately I'm opening up and becoming slightly vulnerable by letting you into my childhood. I'm introducing you to my brother and describing a common experience that the majority of us can relate to. This is not an easy way to start a story, but when done right, it can instantly spark curiosity in what you have to say and create an emotional connection between you and your audience. When it's done badly, it will come across as manipulative or really dull. No doubt you have heard many examples of this in your time. Tread this line carefully, but when you nail it, it will be an incredibly impactful opening.

Don't you just love going to the cinema? Since I was first taken to the cinema as a small boy, my family and I have always played a game where we have to guess what movie trailers we will be shown before the film starts, with one point for each correct guess. Now, with a family of my own, I play the same game with my children. Depending on the film that we go and see, this game and the trailers can sometimes be the highlight of the trip. In the same way that all movies and TV shows have trailers (there's even awards given every year for the best ones called the Golden Trailer Awards), starting your story with a trailer can really grab attention. This is a relatively simple way to begin but can be highly effective. One of the most famous examples is the theme song to *The Fresh Prince of Bel-Air*.

"Now this is a story all about how,

"My life got flipped, turned upside down.

"And I'd like to take a minute, just sit right there,

"I'll tell you how I became the prince of a town called Bel-Air."

Have you carried on singing the rest of the lyrics? Me too.

This is the perfect example of a story trailer because it tells you what it's going to tell you. It hooks you in because you want to know how Will became the prince of Bel-Air.

When it happens in an actual film or show, it's called a 'cold open'. If you've seen *The Hangover*, you'll remember that it starts with Phil, claw marks on his neck and a bleeding lip, standing in the middle of the desert with three-quarters of the 'Wolfpack' behind him leaning on a battered car, calling the stressed-out bride-to-be to tell her that they've lost the groom in Las Vegas five hours before the wedding.

Then the credits start. This is a brilliant way to start a film. Think of all the questions it raises. Why is Phil in such bad shape? What animal left the scratches on his neck? Why are they in the desert? What happened to the car? What happened in Vegas? And how much trouble are they going to be in when he gets home?

I'm not suggesting you rap your next story, and it may not be as wild as *The Hangover*, but something like, "I'm going to tell you the story of how I helped one of our clients increase their turnover by 400 percent in less than three months," or "Let me tell you the story of how I supported our sales team to increase productivity by fifty percent in just two weeks." These are powerful beginnings to a story. Who would switch off at this point and not want to hear how these stories pan out?

These can be pepped up with your use of pictorial language as we discussed above, but with slightly different words. Explore, discover and share are powerful terms to use in your opening sentence because they create action in the mind's eye of your audience. Let's see the difference they make in two examples.

"I'm going to *share* with you the story of how I helped one of our clients increase their turnover by 400 percent in less than three months."

"Let's *explore* together the story of how I supported our sales team to increase productivity by fifty percent in just two weeks."

From these examples, we can see that there's a BIG difference in what's going on in the subconscious of your audience by changing one word.

We talked in the previous chapter about DISC profiles. All the above ideas work really well at the start of your story because they talk directly to the Ds and the Is, so they hook them in straight away because of their ability to think quickly. And everybody, regardless of whether they are D, I, S or C, likes everything I've talked about above. You don't have to be a D to like a great opening action sequence. It will most likely attract the attention of the I, S and C members of your audience too; as a worst-case scenario, it certainly won't offend them.

However, if you start with all the detail and lots of background, you're going to turn off a significant proportion of your audience straight away.

After you've grabbed the attention of your audience, you can tell a part of the story that's going to appeal to the Is and Cs. Who are the people involved and how do the relationships work? And then you can move on to the detail, but no more than is absolutely necessary. Often, particularly in a business story, the detail can be, "if you'd like to know more, click this link/send me an email/

ask me at the end." This means that all the detail is available for those that want it but it doesn't weigh the story down and get in the way of holding the attention of the majority of your audience.

Success Tasks

- Watch the Blake scene from *Glengarry Glen Ross* (it can be found on YouTube) or for that matter, watch the whole film.
- Write five opening lines for your story that start in on the action.
- Write five questions that could work well at the beginning of your story.
- Again, find five ways to open your story provocatively.
- Find five ways to start your story using pictorial language.
- Find five ways to start your story from an emotional place.
- Write a trailer for your story.

Chapter 5: Story Structure

"In the first act get your principal character up a tree; In the second act, throw stones at him; in the third, get him down gracefully."

– George Abbott, theatre producer and director

In school, you were no doubt taught that a story has a beginning, a middle and an end (in literary theory these are called protasis, epitasis and catastrophe). While this is true, it's the two turning points that a story hangs on that are the most important. It's these turning points that give us our beginning, middle and end.

Let me explain.

At the beginning of our story, our character or characters are in their natural state. Everything in their world is as it is, good or bad, with nothing rocking the boat. Then, an inciting incident happens that pushes the character(s) to a point of no return (turning point one). This turns their world 180-degrees, flipping it on its head; throughout the middle of the story, the stakes are raised and the action increases. More often than not, the main character is put through hell until turning point two, when the world is flipped on its head again, which takes us into the end of the story and the resolution, good or bad, happy or sad.

Let's have a look at an example.

In *The Matrix*, Thomas Anderson (Neo) is a programmer and hacker. His job leaves him unsatisfied and he is constantly questioning the world around him, believing that there is more to life. When he is offered the choice to find out the truth about life and leave behind the world he knows forever by swallowing a red pill, or to continue to live a 'normal life' by swallowing a blue pill, he takes the red pill and enters the real world; a dystopian, computerised world completely different from 'the Matrix' that he has been living in, passing the point of no return (turning point one).

The stakes are then raised over and over again as the action rises, including Neo receiving superhuman powers and Morpheus being captured in the Matrix by the bad guys who are hacking into Morpheus' mind to retrieve codes that, if successful, will result in the last human city being destroyed. Neo and his new friend Trinity decide to go back into the Matrix and save Morpheus, which Morpheus and Trinity then escape (turning point two).

After a final climatic battle, all turns out well for Neo, Morpheus and Trinity, and the world and the Matrix are saved.

So, there you have it, *The Matrix* in three parts – beginning, middle and end, hanging on two turning points; Neo taking the red pill, and Neo and Trinity saving Morpheus.

But actually when we look at the story of *The Matrix*, there's more to it than two turning points breaking it into a beginning, middle and end. Let's look at it more closely.

We've got the setup. Thomas Anderson (Neo) is a programmer and hacker. His job leaves him unsatisfied and he is constantly questioning the world around him, believing that there is more to life. Neo's computer is hacked and the text "Wake up, Neo..." appears on his screen. He's told that if he wants to learn more about the Matrix, then he should follow the white rabbit. Suddenly, there's a knock at his door. It's one of his hacking customers who invites him to go clubbing. At first, Neo refuses, until he spots the tattoo of a white rabbit on his customer's girlfriend's shoulder. He goes to the club where he meets Trinity, who explains that he's in danger.

Then there's the inciting incident, the incident that sets the whole story in motion. The next day at work, a package containing a phone is delivered to Neo. When it rings, Morpheus is on the other line. He tells Neo that he's in danger. As agents come to arrest him for his hacking crimes, Morpheus tries to help him escape, but instead Neo allows himself to be arrested rather than attempting to get away.

This is then followed by the point of no return, which is exactly what it sounds like. Once the hero makes a certain decision, they can't turn back. In *The Matrix*, this is where Trinity rescues Neo and takes him to Morpheus where he is offered the choice to find out the truth and leave behind the world he knows forever by swallowing a red pill, or to forget everything Morpheus has told him and continue to live a 'normal life' by swallowing a blue pill. He takes the red pill and enters the real world, passing the point of no return.

This all takes us to turning point one. So, in this model, just the beginning can be broken down into three parts – setup, inciting incident and point of no return (or turning point one).

Let's take a look at the middle – first, rising action. Neo wakes up in the real world and meets the crew of Morpheus' ship, the Nebuchadnezzar. Once he has gained muscle mass, he is trained and tested by the crew so that Morpheus can ascertain if he is indeed 'The One' – the only person who can destroy the Matrix and free humanity. Morpheus tells Neo he believes that Neo is The One. Neo rejects the idea. Morpheus explains that in the Matrix they are being tracked by deadly agents, and that if he dies in the Matrix he will die in the real world. Neo has stepped up to become the badass Morpheus trained him to be, but he and his team are betrayed by a member of their crew and their ship is attacked while they can't defend themselves. Meanwhile in the Matrix, all hell is breaking loose.

Then we come to the midpoint. This is crucial and is a kind of a sub-turning point. At the midpoint, the main character generally comes to a realisation of what they need to do or what is required of them. Whilst in the Matrix, Morpheus takes Neo to meet the Oracle, who confirms the prophesy that Neo is The One. She says that Morpheus is willing to sacrifice his life for his belief that Neo is The One, and that either Neo or Morpheus will die.

Turning point two: Neo and the crew are ambushed by agents and tactical police. Morpheus is captured and the agents begin hacking into Morpheus' mind to retrieve the Zion computers' mainframe codes. If successful, the last human city will be destroyed. Neo's confidence in his abilities grows and he considers if he truly is The One. Neo and Trinity decide to go back into the Matrix and save Morpheus, and Morpheus and Trinity escape the Matrix.

So again, that's three major parts to the middle of the story that will keep it moving along – rising action, midpoint and turning point two.

Let's take a look at the end of the story; first, the 'dark night of the soul'. This is where everything is going wrong for our hero. The crew member who betrayed Morpheus exits the Matrix first. He kills many other crew members that lie defenceless within the real world. As he is about to kill Neo, Tank, a surviving crew member, kills him. The sentinels attack and breach the hull of the Nebuchadnezzar, leaving Neo stuck in the Matrix. He comes face-to-face with Agent Smith, the head of the deadly agents, but fails to kill him, having instead to run away and look for an alternative way to get back into the real world. Neo hears a ringing phone and thinks he's found a way out, but Agent Smith ambushes him and shoots him multiple times, killing him.

The climax is the most intense, exciting or important part of the story. In the real world, Trinity tells Neo while he's plugged into the machine that he can't be dead because she knows she will fall in love with The One, because the Oracle told her so. She kisses him. Neo wakes up from the dead and with his new life comes the power to see and control the Matrix. He defeats Agent Smith.

Then comes the denouement (a posh way of saying epilogue, which in itself is a posh way of saying wrapping everything up). Neo then sends a message to the machines that he's going to wake up everybody that's trapped in the Matrix and flies into the sky.

Once more, this section of the story has three parts – dark night of the soul, climax and denouement.

So actually there are nine story beats within the three-act structure. By looking at the beginning, middle and end in this way, it keeps our action moving along rather than stalling at any point in the story.

We can then break this down further into the hero's journey archetype, or the monomyth, a term coined by Joseph Campbell in his book 'The Hero with a Thousand Faces'. Campbell studied numerous myths and religions in history and found that they had the same seventeen story beats in them. Many of the great films, books and plays that have stood the test of time follow the hero's journey. In 2007, screenwriter Christopher Vogler refined Campbell's original structure in his book 'The Writer's Journey: Mythic Structure for Writers'. This combined a couple of the vaguer elements of the hero's journey and made them a little more tangible. Let's have a look at how *The Matrix* hits Vogler's twelve beats of the hero's journey.

The Ordinary World is where the hero is seen in their everyday life. In *The Matrix*, this is Thomas Anderson's (Neo's) dissatisfaction and constant questioning of the world he lives in.

The Call to Adventure, as with the other two simpler models that we've looked at, is the inciting incident of the story. Neo's computer is hacked and the text "Wake up, Neo..." appears on his screen. He's told that if he wants to learn more about the Matrix, then he should follow the white rabbit. There's a knock at his door and one of his hacking customers invites him to go clubbing.

The Refusal of the Call is where the hero experiences some hesitation to answer the call. At first, Neo refuses to go clubbing until he spots the tattoo of a white rabbit on his customer's girlfriend's shoulder. He goes to the club where he meets Trinity, who explains that he's in danger.

Meeting the Mentor is where the hero gains the supplies, knowledge and confidence needed to start their adventure. In *The Matrix*, this is where the next day at work, a package containing a phone is delivered to Neo. When it rings, Morpheus is on the other line and tells Neo that he's in danger. As the agents come to arrest him for his hacking crimes, Morpheus tries to help him escape, but instead Neo allows himself to be arrested.

This is also a second Refusal of the Call.

Crossing the Threshold is the opposite of The Refusal of the Call where the hero commits wholeheartedly to the adventure; this is when Trinity rescues Neo and takes him to Morpheus, where he is offered the choice between the blue and red pills. He takes the red pill and enters the real world, passing the point of no return.

Tests, Allies and Enemies is where the hero explores the special world (that being the world different to The Ordinary World where they started), faces trials and makes friends and enemies. Neo wakes up in the real world and meets the crew of the Nebuchadnezzar. He's trained, told by Morpheus that he believes that Neo is The One, and is told that in the Matrix they are being tracked by deadly agents and that if he dies in the Matrix, he will die in the real world. The team are betrayed by a member of their crew and their ship is attacked while they can't defend themselves, whilst in the Matrix all hell is breaking loose.

The Approach to the Innermost Cave – here the hero nears the centre of the story and the special world. Whilst in the Matrix, Morpheus takes Neo to meet the Oracle who confirms the prophesy that Neo is The One. She says that Morpheus is willing to sacrifice his life for his belief that Neo is The One, and that either Neo or Morpheus will die.

The Ordeal is where the hero faces their greatest challenge yet and experiences death and rebirth. This is not usually a physical death and rebirth but often a life crisis, spiritual or philosophical death and rebirth. In *The Matrix*, Neo and the crew are ambushed by agents and tactical police. Morpheus is captured and the agents hack into Morpheus' mind to retrieve the Zion computers' mainframe codes. If successful, the last human city will be destroyed.

The Reward is where the hero experiences the consequences of surviving 'death'. They seize a metaphorical 'sword', be it a physical item or a piece of wisdom or knowledge that allows them to persevere, which helps them to take on their biggest challenge yet. In *The Matrix*, Neo's confidence in his abilities grow and he considers if he truly is The One. Neo and Trinity decide to go back into the Matrix and save Morpheus, and Morpheus and Trinity escape the Matrix.

The Road Back is where the hero sees a light at the end of the tunnel and either returns to The Ordinary World or continues to an ultimate destination. In the film, the crew member who betrayed Morpheus exits the Matrix first. He kills many crew members that lie defenceless within the real world. As he is about to kill Neo, Tank, a surviving crew member, kills him.

The sentinels attack and breach the hull of the Nebuchadnezzar, leaving Neo stuck in the Matrix. He comes face-to-face with Agent Smith but fails to kill him, having instead to run away and look for an alternative way to get back into the real world.

The Resurrection is the climax of the film. The hero faces their final test and resolves all the conflict that they've faced. The hero experiences a final moment of death and rebirth, so they are pure when they re-enter The Ordinary World. Neo hears a ringing phone and thinks he's found a way out, but Agent Smith ambushes him and shoots him multiple times, killing him. In the real world, Trinity tells him that he can't be dead because she knows she will fall in love with The One, because the Oracle told her so. She kisses him. Neo wakes up from the dead, and with his new life comes the power to see and control the Matrix. He defeats Agent Smith.

Return with the Elixir is where the hero returns with something to improve The Ordinary World. In *The Matrix*, Neo sends a message to the machines that he's going to wake up everybody that's trapped in the Matrix and flies into the sky.

So, there you have it. You'll never watch a movie or read a book in the same way again, and I do apologise. My friend Andy says I've ruined movies forever for him, because rather than sitting and allowing a film to wash over him and thinking everything will turn out ok in the end, he can work out what's coming next because of these structures.

But why do these structures work?

They work because we've been trained to understand this story structure for as long as stories have been told.

Joseph Campbell studied hundreds if not thousands of stories, myths and religions to write his book and his theory of the monomyth, and they all follow the same structure. We love to hear stories that follow this pattern (as we discussed in Chapter One, the brain loves patterns), which is why the most successful films of all time are so beloved. Think *Star Wars*, *Indiana Jones* or *The Godfather* – they all follow this structure.

If you can use this structure or at least be aware of it when you are crafting your stories, your words will really connect and resonate.

It's also well known by screenwriters that the middle of your story is where you're most likely to lose your audience. You've spent all your time and effort working out how your story ends with a gigantic climax and you've put tonnes of effort into grabbing your audience's attention by starting right in on the action. So how do you keep your audience engaged throughout the middle of the story that is typically as long as the set up and the climax combined? Primarily, it's this structure that's going to help.

For example, think about the midpoint. By this stage in the story, we're starting to run out of energy and we need a little bit more fuel on the fire, so the storyteller needs to raise the stakes by making the whole adventure more meaningful and important to them. This adds fuel to the audience's engagement because when we know that the story means more to the main character, it suddenly means more the audience.

In *The Matrix*, the midpoint is when the Oracle tells Neo that either he will die or that Morpheus will sacrifice his life so that Neo can live. Talk about raising the stakes and causing the main character to invest more into their story. It certainly re-engages the audience if they've started to disengage.

If we think about it, most business case studies tend to follow this pattern anyway.

Roughly, a business is sat in stasis (usually bad) until an outside business comes along to help them. Initially, they don't want the help. Then they meet the person in the outside business who can help them. Eventually, they agree to be helped and cross the threshold. Then come the challenges of making changes. They get to the point where they understand what must be done and experience a business rebirth into new understanding, coming out the other side with fresh wisdom and knowledge. They continue to their final destination, resolve the initial conflict from the start of the story and improve their world.

Sound familiar?

There are your twelve beats of the hero's journey in a very compressed business story, and the best-case studies include all twelve beats. Some that I've read tend closer to nine and most, if I'm being honest, include only a beginning, middle and end.

We've just looked at how stories are structured, the hero's journey, and how that fits into our story. I'm sure that you can see from this that the biblical writer of the Book of Ecclesiastes was correct when he stated that, "there is nothing new under the sun."

If you were to visit the British Library, you would find approximately twenty-five million books. That's more books than in any other library in the world, with some dating back as far as 300BC. However, in all twenty-five million of these books, there are only considered to be seven stories.

In his 2004 book 'The Seven Basic Plots: Why we tell stories', Christopher Booker summarised these seven main story arcs that make up all storytelling throughout the ages as follows: Overcoming the Monster, Rags to Riches, The Quest, Voyage and Return, Comedy, Tragedy and Rebirth.

Let's start with Overcoming the Monster. This is where the hero has to defeat a force that opposes them. A good example of this is *Star Wars* where the hero, Luke Skywalker, must overcome the forces of the Empire and Darth Vader that threaten both the rebels he supports and him personally. Other examples include *Seven Samurai*, *The Magnificent Seven* (the same film, just set in the Wild West) and *Jaws*. Secondly, Rags to Riches, as demonstrated really well in *Cinderella*, *Aladdin* and most of the stories written by Charles Dickens where, as the name suggests, the hero starts out poor and comes into money, fame and/or power, and love. Subsequently, they lose it all and become a better person because of it, often regaining the wealth, power or love at the end.

The third story arc is The Quest where again, as the name suggests, the hero and often a bunch of ragtag companions set out on a quest to discover something, somewhere or someone, overcoming obstacles and temptations along the way and ultimately finding themselves as they go. *The Lord of the Rings*, *Raiders of the Lost Ark* and *Monty Python and the Holy Grail* are great examples of this story arc.

Next up is Voyage and Return – think *Alice in Wonderland*, *The Lion King* and *Back to the Future*, where the hero visits a strange world, learns lessons, overcomes obstacles and threats, and returns home with a new way of thinking.

The fifth story arc is Comedy, where the hero meets a happy ending but not before experiencing a series of confusing and often comedic events. This is more than humour, with the emphasis placed on the triumph over the confusion. However, more often than not, it is humorous and always results in a happy ending. Most romances, unless there's a tragic ending, will find their way into this story arc. Good examples include *Four Weddings and a Funeral*, *The Big Lebowski* and *Bridget Jones's Diary*.

Tragedy is the opposite of Comedy, where the flawed hero meets a tragic end thanks to a series of mistakes and bad choices that they make. Because they are inherently a good character, we feel empathy with their eventual downfall. Think *Romeo and Juliet*, *Bonnie and Clyde* and *Citizen Kane*.

Rebirth rounds off the list. Here, the hero experiences an event or a series of events that transform them into a better person. In

'A Christmas Carol', for example, Ebenezer Scrooge is forced to see his past, present and future lives by the ghosts that he meets, forcing him to change his ways. A similar story arc happens in the films *Groundhog Day* and *Beauty and the Beast*.

As with everything, there will be the exceptions that prove the rule, but in the main, these arcs are not a bad way of starting to plan your storytelling. Roughly, what arc does the story that you are telling fit into? Is it a Rags to Riches story or a Rebirth story? Take a look at one of the examples mentioned that goes along with your story arc, say *Cinderella*, and see if you can match the story beats with those in your own story.

You will also notice that all the seven story arcs follow the three story structures that we looked at in the previous chapter; they all have a beginning, a middle and an end, they all hit all nine story beats, and they all hit all twelve beats of the hero's journey, once again proving how important story structure is.

Success Tasks

- Watch *The Matrix* with this chapter open to see where these moments happen.
- Watch one other film and see if you can work out where each of the moments happen for each of the three models (two turning points, nine plot points and twelve plot points). An action/adventure film will be pretty easy, or stretch yourself and try it with something more comedy-, romance- or drama-based.
- Write the beats out for your story for each of these

three models.

- Think back to the last ten films or TV shows you've watched. What story arc did they each fit into?
- How about the last novel you read? What story arc did that fit into?
- Which story arc does your story fit into? Write out your story following one of the examples within your respective story arc.

Chapter 6: So What?

"Wherever we want to go, we go. That's what a ship
is, you know. It's not just a keel and hull and a deck
and sails. That's what a ship needs. But what a ship is,
what the Black Pearl really is, is freedom."

– Captain Jack Sparrow, Pirates of the Caribbean:
The Curse of the Black Pearl

A very wise man – Theodore Levitt, economist and professor
at the Harvard Business School – once said that, "People don't
want quarter-inch drill bits. They want quarter-inch holes." I know
the point he's making. But who in their right mind wants quarter-
inch holes dotted all around their house?

I am being a tad facetious, but I don't think Herr Levitt went far
enough with his analogy. The reason people buy quarter-inch drill
bits is to drill quarter-inch holes to insert quarter-inch screws to
hang picture frames that contain photos of loved ones or events
in order to evoke treasured memories and make us feel warm
and fuzzy inside.

That's why I like Captain Sparrow's analogy better. He explains
the benefits and how they are much more than the features.
Granted, it's not as pithy as old Teddy's famous quote, but I
think it gets the point across more thoroughly. And all while he's
intoxicated and stranded on a desert island with a very angry
Elizabeth Swann.

In his book 'The Jelly Effect: How to Make Your Communication
Stick', Andy Bounds takes features and benefits one step further.

He says, "Customers don't care what you do. They only care what they're left with after you've done it."

So, if you design websites, your customers don't care that you design websites, they only care what they get as a result of buying one of your websites. They should get a website that looks good and is well optimised, which means more people will see it and stay on it. As a result – the 'afters' as Andy Bounds puts it – their sales will go up. They've not come to you as the web developer to get a website, they've come to you because they want more sales.

If you work in IT, customers don't come to you because they want to buy a computer or some cabling. They come to you because they want to be more efficient. The 'afters' is how you enable them to be more efficient.

If you are an optician, you aren't selling glasses, you're selling vision (and hopefully style).

Steve Jobs had it right. The iPod wasn't one GB of storage for your MP3s. It was one thousand songs in your pocket.

In Andy's words, "Nobody wants what you do, they want what you cause." Or in the words of Andrew Gibson, author of 'What's Your URP?', "What difference does what you're selling make in the lives of your clients?"

Remember that people are motivated to buy into anything, be it a product, service or idea, for one of two reasons – to prevent a pain or to achieve a goal. The majority of people tend to be motivated by benefits that prevent pain, and a minority of people are motivated by what they stand to gain from the benefits. The key difference between pain and gain is that benefits that lead to gains can easily be put off because the outcomes are never urgent – they will always be eclipsed by the pain prevention benefits. So it's important that when you're thinking about the benefits and afters that you have to offer, you list both pain prevention and gain benefits.

When you're planning what story to tell, it's vital to know what benefits your target audience require and that you have the right story to tell that includes those benefits.

Have you ever been in the situation where you've sat through a story and, regardless of how delightfully told it was, as the story concludes you wonder to yourself just what the point of the story was?

That's because the benefit behind the story was not well thought out or planned sufficiently before the story commenced, and often the wrong story is told for the situation.

As we discussed in Chapter Three on beginning with the end in mind, I find that often the whole process needs to be reverse engineered, starting with the desired outcome. If we know what outcome we want to achieve from the situation, be it a sale, getting your team behind your idea or winning a negotiation, then we can work out the right story to tell.

Once we know this, we can write down the benefits or afters of achieving this outcome. Try to get a list of at least ten, even if that is difficult, because it gets the creative juices flowing. And try and make sure that you have a mix of both pain prevention and gain benefits. Keep writing until you have ten because the last two or three are either complete garbage or completely genius ideas. These have to be real benefits or afters, like we've just talked about; not what the ship needs but what the ship is.

At this stage, forget about the desired outcome completely.

You should only be interested in the benefits that you've listed. For each benefit, think about a time that you've delivered that benefit before, or a story you've heard where someone else has delivered that benefit, or a metaphor or allegory (more on this later) that is suitable for the situation.

By doing this for each benefit, you will have a list of up to ten stories at your disposal for the situation that you're going into, all of which, when told well, will lead you and those you share it with to your desired outcome.

Success Tasks

- Check your diary for your next three meetings. What are your desired outcomes for these meetings?
- List ten benefits for each of these outcomes. Make sure to include pain prevention and gain benefits.
- Work out what story is suitable for each of these benefits, be it a story you've been involved in, a story you've heard, or a metaphor or allegory.
- Take a look at the story you tell regularly. Are you using it in the right context with the right benefits for the right audience?

The Human Element

Chapter 7: Emotion

"I've learned that people will forget what you said, people will forget what you did, but people will never forget how you made them feel."

— Maya Angelou, poet and civil rights activist

Stories are inherently emotional. We've seen already the plot points that characters go through in a story and the fact that the best stories put their characters through hell and turmoil before they reach any form of resolution. The reason that this works so well is because we are emotional beings and we connect with and learn alongside the characters in these stories as they go. Our empathy kicks in and we feel our way through the story with the characters when it's told well.

When you ask people what their favourite film is, I'm sure that you regularly get the same answer that I get from many of the people that I speak to – *The Shawshank Redemption*. It also sits at the top of IMDb's Top 250 films of all time. And there's a good reason for this. It gets you right where you feel it. You feel your way through the film with Red and Andy, and it never once becomes an intellectual exercise.

Are there better films? Possibly.

Sitting just below it at number two on IMDb's Top 250 films of all time is *The Godfather*, with *The Godfather Part II* at number three. It could certainly be argued that both these films are better than *The Shawshank Redemption*, but are they as consistently emotive? I think this is the reason that they've been pipped to the post in the IMDb ranking, and probably in the number of times you get told that *The Shawshank Redemption* is someone's favourite film.

As is the case in *The Shawshank Redemption*, emotion in stories only truly works when there are swings and shifts through the emotional spectrum. If the emotion is perpetually sad, then you come out of the experience depressed. If it's permanently happy, the cheeriness begins to lose its efficacy and the whole experience becomes rather bland.

It's the films that swing and shift through the emotional spectrum that create a physical emotional reaction in us and cause them to stay lodged in our memory because of this.

Believe it or not, there are three different types of tears – basal tears, reflex tears and emotional tears. Emotional tears, which are those laced with endorphins (chemicals produced by the body to relieve stress and pain), tend to flow during times when you feel a loss of control, such as when a story has taken you on an emotional rollercoaster and leads you to breakdown at the emotional climax. These tears, along with increased heartrate and slower breathing, work together to take back control of your emotions and stabilise your mood but in doing so cause a lump to form in your throat.

Two of my favourite TV shows are really great examples of how stories can swing and shift through the emotional spectrum in order to have an emotional impact on their audience. One is a comedy, *Scrubs*, and one is a drama, *The West Wing*. *Scrubs* has a tendency to go from very silly and goofy one minute to serious, sad and life-affirming the next, thus making the comedy funnier and the serious aspects more emotive. *The West Wing* does the opposite. It can go from very intense one minute to very funny and witty the next, making the drama more dramatic and the humour more entertaining. There are many examples of this throughout both shows because they are exceptionally well written, produced and directed – probably the best comedy and drama to have ever graced our screens. Let me give you an example from each.

In the *Scrubs* episode called 'My Last Chance', there's a whole zany storyline going on about JD needing a permission slip from Elliot to sleep with Molly, JD being kidnapped and abandoned in the middle of nowhere by the janitor, his phone being stolen by a coyote, Turk trying to help only to make things worse, and JD finally being turned down by Molly after being given a trick permission slip by Elliot. As I say, pretty zany and very funny.

Whilst all that hilarity is ensuing, Dr Cox is forced to spend two back-to-back twelve-hour shifts in an ambulance with an incredibly irritating EMT called Denise in order to complete his community service. Dr Cox being Dr Cox is immediately infuriated by her annoying rambling and the conflict starts, as does a great deal of the storyline's humour.

Early on in their riding around together, Denise draws Dr Cox's attention to a photo of her son on the dashboard, saying that he is ten years old in the picture and that he'll always be that age to her.

The next day, Denise shows up at Dr Cox's apartment before his second shift. She tells him and his wife Jordan about her son's favourite Ken Griffey Jr baseball card, saying that he always carries it on him wherever he goes. During his second shift, Dr Cox sits in the back of the ambulance to try and ignore Denise, and whilst trying to engage with Dr Cox from the front, Denise crashes the ambulance and breaks her collarbone.

Whilst Denise is being treated in the hospital, Dr Cox gets her to sign his community service form. Once he's got what he came for, he releases all his pent-up frustration about how irritating she is in a brutally honest and somewhat amusing tirade. As he leaves the room, an orderly asks him if he left anything in the ambulance and hands him a Ken Griffey Jr baseball card. Piecing everything together, Dr Cox realises that Denise's son is dead. With his humanity returning, he goes back into the room and learns that her son was killed in an accident, which is why she learnt to be a paramedic.

This episode gets me every time. Even now, having seen it goodness knows how many times, I still feel a lump in my throat and a tear in my eye when Denise starts telling Dr Cox about how great the paramedics were with her son. It's the way that one minute I'm laughing along with JD and Turk, the next I'm empathising with Dr Cox about how irritating Denise is, then – bam! It hits me with the realisation of the fact that she is grieving the loss of her son and is so very lonely and just wants someone to talk to since her son died. And yet the whole episode, I've been laughing at how unkind Dr Cox has been to her. The toing and froing of the storylines and the emotional arcs of the characters really do a number on the audience.

It's the same with *The West Wing* episode. In fact, I watched it again recently having forgotten what was about to happen and it was like someone had punched me in the stomach, it was that powerful. I don't need to say it because everyone else does, but that's just how good a writer Aaron Sorkin is.

In *The West Wing* Season One Christmas episode 'In Excelsis

Deo', Josh and Sam are worried that a congressman may leak some secrets about their good friend and boss, Leo, so they approach Sam's prostitute friend to dig up dirt to use as leverage against the congressman's allies. They do so against the express wishes of Leo. CJ becomes emotionally involved in a hate crime story that no one else shows any interest in, but this leads to a great deal of flirting with White House reporter Danny. Donna constantly pesters Josh about her Christmas present, and whilst he doesn't get her what she asked for, she is delighted with his final choice. President Bartlet sneaks out to go shopping at a rare book shop and won't allow PR executive Mandy to take some photographers with her, which winds her up no end.

Whilst all this is happening, Toby gets called by the police to identify a dead homeless man. It turns out that the man, who was a Korean war veteran, was wearing a coat that Toby donated to Goodwill and Toby had left his business card in it. This saddens him, so he tracks down the dead man's brother, who is also homeless.

In the middle of all this is a small scene where Charlie asks Mrs Landingham, the president's assistant, if she's feeling ok. She says that at Christmas she misses her twin boys, who were killed in Vietnam. It's a very short interchange and seems like an incidental scene thrown into the middle of all the chaos and fun of Josh, Sam, CJ, Danny, Donna and the president, but it hits like an emotional punch to the stomach, particularly when she says, "they were so young… it's hard when something like that happens so far away because they had to be so scared. It's hard not to think that right then they needed their mother."

Using the influence of the president's name, Toby arranges a military funeral at Arlington National Cemetery. The president is told about Toby's stunt and Toby thinks he's in for a world of pain. But the president can only muster limited exasperation and asks if Toby, again using the president's name, has taken the USA out of NATO. This conversation between Toby and the president lifts the whole mood of the preceding ten minutes and brings some much needed humour. Toby leaves the Oval Office to head to the funeral, only to find Mrs Landingham waiting for him, dressed in black. She simply says, "Toby, I'd like to come along." And that's the one-two punch. At that point, I just burst into tears. And I mean explode. Such a simple line set up ten minutes earlier by a tragic ninety second monologue, interspersed by drama, comedy and romance. It's perfect.

Mrs Landingham goes to the funeral with Toby and all the cast then meet back at the White House for some carol singing, so that the audience can finish with a warm feeling of completion.

With both episodes, there is nothing manipulative about the emotional climax, and this is really important. There's no swelling music. The emotional punch isn't overplayed. In fact, it's delivered very matter-of-factly in both cases. It just is what it is.

Watching the climax scenes on their own would undoubtedly have some emotional impact, but it's what comes before them that makes them so effective. It's the interplay of swinging from one emotion to the other that has such a powerful effect on the audience.

In business, we are too often afraid to get emotional for fear that people will see us as out of place. Actually, I think if we bring emotion into the business environment, be it a sales situation, presentation or a team meeting, it probably is a little unusual and will make us stand out, and done authentically, it can make a big difference to the outcome that we want.

Why do I say done well? Because, usually, when it is done, it's done inauthentically and manipulatively. How many times have you sat in a presentation and felt manipulated as someone has used a painful experience to try to sell something? Or you've read a LinkedIn post where someone has shoehorned in a story to fit a point they're trying to make? Or you've cringed at a TV advert, which has been so misjudged that all the emotion is so overblown and you feel used afterwards.

I have a confession to make, and you may think less of me once I reveal this to you. I hate – and I mean *hate* – Christmas TV adverts. They are the most saccharine, syrupy, cringy, emotionally manipulative pieces of sales content you are ever likely to come across. They take all our warm fuzzy feelings at a time when we tend to be at our most vulnerable and are already looking through rose-tinted spectacles and squeeze out the last drop of emotion with a crappy, cloying cover of an already awful pop song playing over the top, all in order to sell us garbage that we don't need. There's usually a cute, animated critter looking for its family who are all tucked up warm in their nest, or a rocking horse next to a giant, brightly lit Christmas tree, or beautiful people kissing each other in romantic settings. And there's always snow! Sorry, I went into a white rage there and lost control. I'm back.

However, I have found one Christmas advert that I really like, and it's because it's the opposite of all these things (apart from the snow). Firstly, it meets the audience where they are rather than attempting to be overly sentimental and forcing the emotion upon them. Secondly, the music stays virtually consistent throughout, not demanding that the audience feel a certain way. Thirdly, Christmas is never mentioned, there is just the odd Christmas tree in the background. Fourthly, in the whole advert, the company are on the screen for less than three seconds across three separate shots.

In the same way that both *Scrubs* and *The West Wing* shift the emotion one way then the next and don't overplay their hand, this advert works because it does the same. The advert is the 2020 UK Amazon Christmas advert that follows the ballet dancer whose performance is cancelled because of the Coronavirus pandemic.

When it comes to telling your story, it's about striking the right balance of emotion, swinging and shifting just enough but not overdoing it to the point of manipulation.

There are two tiers of emotions – primary emotions and secondary emotions. The primary emotions are brief, intense and cannot be controlled: they are anger, disgust, fear, happiness, sadness and surprise.

The secondary emotions are love, guilt, shame, pride, envy and jealousy. What is immediately apparent to me about the secondary emotions is how social they are and how important they are. You can feel the primary emotions by yourself, but the secondary emotions can only be felt with or towards someone else. Are these so-called secondary emotions secondary in reality? Without them, we wouldn't be able to form human relationships, which seems pretty fundamental to me. And what is the most fundamental of all the emotions? Love, of course.

At this stage in your story planning process, you need to work out how each of your major characters is feeling at each of your major plot points. Of course, this can be a mix of emotions, but more often than not there's likely to be one that is stronger than the rest.

It's a good idea to work up a plot point/emotion matrix to help you work this out. A simple spreadsheet can help with this. In the first column, write out each of your plot points, then across the top row, write out each of your major characters' names. In each corresponding box, simply write down how the character was feeling. You'll soon get a good idea of your characters' emotional arcs and how their arcs interact with the characters around them. I have created a simple plot point/emotion matrix that you can download at www.weareopusmedia.com/ruletheworld to help you get started.

Let's take *The Matrix* as an example. If we jump a little way into the story to The Road Back plot point, Neo feels fear, Trinity feels sadness and Morpheus feels anger. As they reach The Resurrection, Neo then feels surprise, Trinity feels love and Morpheus feels pride. All the characters switch from negative to positive emotions, giving us that emotional switch in the audience, but all the character emotions are different so that we get a rich tapestry of characters for a more enjoyable and interesting cinematic experience.

Success Tasks

- Watch *Scrubs* Season Four, Episode Eight: 'My Last Chance'.
- Watch *The West Wing* Season One, Episode Ten: 'In Excelsis Deo'.

- Watch a bunch of Christmas TV adverts, including the 2020 UK Amazon advert entitled 'The Show Must Go On'.
- Write up your plot point/emotion matrix for your story.

Chapter 8: Who's the Hero?

"Focusing on the customer makes a
company more resilient."
– Jeff Bezos, CEO, Amazon.*"*

I love *The Lord of the Rings*, the films more than the books. I like to wind up my brother, who studied English literature at university, by saying, "Why read the book when I can watch the film?" And whilst I don't believe that to be true at all, and I have read *The Lord of the Rings*, I love how Peter Jackson and his team brought the whole realm of Middle Earth and the characters to life.

I'm a huge fan of Gandalf. I love two things about him in particular. Firstly, I love his authority. I love that when he speaks, all creatures listen. Denethor allows him into the archives at Gondor (albeit begrudgingly), he leads the army of Erkenbrand of Westfold and a hoard of Ents to save Helm's Deep, and he even has authority over the Balrog, so much so that after an eight day battle, he slays the creature, travels out of thought and time, and returns as Gandalf the White.

The second thing I love about Gandalf is his empathy. He has empathy for Frodo in the Mines of Moria when Frodo is at his lowest ebb, for Pippin on the precipice of defeat in war-torn Gondor, and even for Gollum, suggesting at one point to Frodo that he should have more compassion for him. After all, Gollum was once a Hobbit before his life took a turn for the worse.

On numerous occasions, Gandalf also calls Frodo and the rest of the fellowship to action. The first time he does this is in Bag End, Frodo's home, when he tells Frodo that the ring can't stay in the Shire and he must head for the Inn of the Prancing Pony at the village of Bree. By his actions in supporting Frodo, he then calls the rest of the fellowship to join the adventure at the Council of Elrond at Rivendell.

During one of Frodo's lowest ebbs when he says he wishes he had never found the ring and for none of the adventure to ever have happened, Gandalf delivers some of the wisest words of encouragement ever written that are also a call to action – "So do all who live to see such times; but that is not for them to decide. All we have to decide is what to do with the time that is given to us."

Notice that on each of these occasions, and on all the other times throughout the story where Gandalf calls any of the characters to action, he also gives them a plan. He doesn't just tell them to get on with it; he also helps them with *how* to get on with it.

But is Gandalf the hero of *The Lord of the Rings*? No. Frodo is the hero. Gandalf is what's known as a sage, mentor or supernatural aid. Think back to Chapter Five and the Hero's Journey – this is really key to the story of *The Lord of the Rings*. Never once does Gandalf attempt to become the hero. In fact, on more than one occasion, he is offered the ring and he refuses to take it. He is there to help Frodo to be the hero throughout the story.

This is a good lesson for us when we're working with our clients in general. We need authority and empathy; we need to call them to action and give them a plan. But it is especially important when we are telling stories that involve ourselves that we must NEVER be Frodo and must ALWAYS be Gandalf. In the retelling of your stories, the clients or team members who you help and support must always be Frodo. We must always be looking to make them the hero.

Why?

Well, first of all, no one likes a show-off. How many times have you heard a story, in business or life, where you find yourself thinking you wish the person would just stop because you can't stand the bragging or, worst of all, the humble bragging? You see it on websites, social media and in presentations all the time – "Look at this amazing website we built", "We're amazing at being plumbers", "Top ten law firm in the country". It's just bragging, and actually most of the time a lot of it is unfounded. In the 1950s during the *Mad Men* era, it was the way stuff was sold and punters bought into it. Nowadays, the millennial generation and Gen-Z are much more cynical, and they have seen this stuff so many times before that they don't believe a word of it.

Secondly, by making your prospect or team member the hero of your story rather than yourself, you will honour their journey and their struggle rather than making light of it and making it seem insignificant. In the process, you will honour the journey and struggle of your audience. By constantly making yourself the hero, you will make it seem like everything is easy to overcome and that the people you have helped in the past shouldn't have wasted your time bringing their problems to you. You diminish the obstacle that was overcome. But by making your audience, be it a prospect, client or team member the hero of the story, and by taking the place of their mentor, you can demonstrate authority and empathy, call them to action, and give them a plan that takes them on a journey through the story that will help them to overcome their struggle, making them the hero in the process.

Which leads me to my third point. You create a hero. Frodo wasn't a hero at the start of *The Lord of the Rings*, living in a little Hobbit hole in the Shire. He'd never even left Hobbiton. But a combination of his circumstances and Gandalf's mentoring made a hero out of him, and you can do the same with the protagonist in your story by the way you tell it.

This does an amazing thing for those listening to your story. They see that you've created heroes in the past and they want to be a hero too. I mean, who doesn't want to be a hero? They know that you can make them one, so why wouldn't they want to work with you?

To back this up, here's a little stat for you. According to Deloitte and Touché, hero-making companies are sixty percent more profitable compared to non-hero-making companies.

But how do we translate this into business speak?

Take a look back at Chapter Five and see how this fits into the hero's journey. You can see that the mentor is there, guiding the hero nearly every step of the way, and you will be too in your client's story. You may remember in Chapter Five that I outlined the twelve steps of a business story based on the hero's journey. To save you flicking back, I've included it below.

"Roughly, a business is sat in stasis (usually bad) until an outside business comes along to help them. Initially, they don't want the help. Then they meet the person in the outside business [a mentor] who can help them. Eventually, they agree to be helped and cross the threshold. Then come the challenges of making changes. They get to the point where they understand what must be done and experience a business rebirth into new understanding, coming out the other side with fresh wisdom and knowledge. They continue to their final destination, resolve the initial conflict from the start of the story and improve their world."

Notice that the outside business that comes along to help is the mentor with the call to action. Often it takes a couple of nudges to get them to cross the threshold. These nudges require both authority and empathy. It also requires a plan so that the client knows where they're going and the changes that they need to make. But it is them that need to make the changes. No outside force can go into a business and enforce changes. A good mentor is there every step of the way to ensure that through the struggles, rebirth and arrival at their final destination, they have everything that they need. You've made them the hero in the story as it's the hero's journey, not your journey (you didn't cross a threshold, have many changes to make, or experience a business rebirth). Yet you will still come out smelling like roses, ready to reap the rewards.

Let's look at some examples of hero-making storytelling in action.

We'll start with a bad example. I'm going to pick on a whole industry because it would be unfair to single one firm out and, to be honest, in this industry they're all pretty much as bad as each other. Law firms. Go to any law firm website and look at the story they purport to tell on their Homepage, About page, or any other page on their website for that matter. Who's the hero? They are. When writing this book, I randomly looked at ten law firm websites and here are the things that they regularly talked about on their sites, in no particular order: the year in which they were established (every one), where their offices are based (every one), the types of legal work they do (every one), how many staff they have (nearly all of them), how many years' experience their staff have, their accreditations, who their branch manager is, the fact that they work internationally, the fact that they have a good reputation, the awards they've won, and who their founder was back in 1827.

And every pronoun on every website is 'we'.

Let me ask you a couple of questions. Who's the hero on these websites? A fairly obvious answer. Genuinely, who cares about any of that stuff in the list above? And more importantly, how can these law firms expect to stand out from each other? And how easy would it be as a law firm to stand out by changing the narrative on the website? Just change the pronouns to 'you' and make it about how you help your clients instead of talking about yourself!

So now that I've annoyed the most litigious industry in the world, let's take a look at a good example where a company really got all these elements right in a campaign.

General Mills Honey Nut Cheerios are the most popular cereal in the world, selling more boxes every year than any other brand. They also have other varieties including Original, Fruity and Banana Nut. Since their inception, they have always been a very popular cereal because they make their customers into the hero in all their marketing, from the Superbowl advert where the little girl uses the cereal to take care of her daddy's heart, to floating one cheerio in the toilet bowl to teach toddlers to aim whilst toilet training, to one of my favourite recent ad campaigns that they ran called #HowToDad.

This was a very tongue-in-cheek but well put together ad that was run in Canada. The dad in the ad talks to the camera whilst getting his kids ready for the day. It starts as he is woken up by his son wearing a very creepy leather horse mask, and then proceeds to humorously school the audience regarding what makes an awesome dad, which includes but is not limited to: telling hilarious jokes, building the best forts, doing artwork and homework, discipline, and fixing heartbreak. There's even a line in the ad where he says that kids, "look to us in the same way that we look to superheroes. Up. Because we're taller." The ad finishes with him telling the audience that Peanut Butter Cheerios are the official cereal of 'dadhood'.

Magic!

What dad is not going to love that?

The hero of the advert has connected with dads on every level, talked about all the things he does for his kids that make him a hero to them, and told us that Peanut Butter Cheerios are going to be there for him and his kids. As a dad, I'm sold. And not once did Cheerios talk about the fact that they lower your cholesterol and risk of heart disease, or the fact that they contain several essential nutrients that most people don't get enough of, such as fibre, vitamin D and iron.

So, what's the take away here?

Make your audience into the hero of YOUR story as well as THEIR story, and when these two stories align, you will move them to action.

Success Tasks

- Watch *The Lord of the Rings* or at least some clips of

Gandalf on YouTube (I know they are long films).

- Google search 'solicitors' and try and find one that makes their customers the hero of the story on their website.
- Watch the #HowToDad Peanut Butter Cheerios ad on YouTube.
- Go back over your story and work out who the hero is. If you're involved, is it you or the person you're helping? If it's you, shift it so that the person you're helping becomes the hero and you come across as the mentor with authority and empathy, and that you call them to action and give them a plan, and that you're there throughout the journey, just like Gandalf.

The
11 Cs to
Connect

Chapter 9: Character

"The best stories always end up being
about people rather than the event."
– Stephen King, author

Who is in your story?

That sounds like a really daft question, doesn't it? Of course, we already know the answer to this question. But do we really? We know the characters, but do we really *know* the characters? We need to know our characters inside out in order to paint a full picture so that our audience connects with them, otherwise they will become two-dimensional caricatures that will leave our audience feeling detached.

Stephen King says that, "the best stories always end up being about people rather than the event." Whether it is film, documentary or literature, this is true. Consider stories that take place during true events, from *Titanic* and *Saving Private Ryan*, *The Defiant Ones* and *The Last Dance*, to *War and Peace* and *The Three Musketeers*. Though these events are fascinating, what makes the storytelling so captivating is the characters who are involved and their points of view through which we experience the story. So, when telling our stories, we need to make them about the people in the story and how they felt during the events taking place rather than about the events themselves. If we don't really get to know the characters, then how do we know their world, how they would react, how they are feeling, and what motivates them?

We've covered the events that are happening in the chapter on structure, and what feelings your characters are encountering in the chapter on emotion. In this chapter, we're going to cover how to bring the characters to life at the intersection of event, emotion and physicality.

More often than not, and certainly in a business context, we're telling a story that actually happened, meaning that the characters in our story will be real people. (Of course, on occasion, we may be using an allegory or metaphor where we have to create our character from scratch – more on allegory and metaphor in Chapter Twenty One.) When our characters are real people, we have an advantage because we don't have to create them from our imagination. Chances are we have met them or have at least heard stories about them, so we know who they are. We can always do research into our real characters by speaking with them or studying what others have said about them.

A good place to start with our characters is understanding what their role is in the story. Are they the hero, the mentor, an ally, an enemy or an oracle? Once you know this, you can move on to where they are introduced in the story based on the hero's journey and how you are going to introduce them.

And when you introduce your characters and when you're talking about your characters, use the character's name. It personalises them. But, unless they are famous or it's necessary because they're someone that the audience will know, don't use their full name. It's boring. I'm sure we all have a relative who, when they tell a story, include full names. I'm imagining that these characters are people that we've never met before and are never likely to meet. Character first names will suffice.

There's a clever thing that the brain does when we hear

certain words and descriptions. Take the numbers '9/11' for example. What immediately came to your mind? Strange, isn't it? Essentially, they are two numbers separated by a forward slash on a page. But because of our collective memory, when the numbers are put together like that, we associate them with sounds, images and feelings. This is our subconscious doing the hard work for us. I didn't have to write any more than two numbers and one punctuation mark, and you were immediately transported to a place in time and space.

The same happens when we describe our characters. The subconscious of our audience does the hard work for us. This is why the advice is the same when writing character descriptions: less is more. Keep it short and sweet and to the point. The audience want to see the characters actions and feel their emotions. That's how they're defined, after all.

I was once given some great advice by a screenwriter, which was that when writing character descriptions, I should focus on their hair, clothes and makeup descriptions, or other physical descriptions that foreshadow their character type, and how they enter the scene. That's not to say that you should go into reams of detail; remember, less is more. Let our collective memory do the work. If you can use one sentence (two at a push) to sum up your character, then you're well on your way to doing a great job of describing them and setting them up nicely for your audience and the rest of the story.

With that in mind, below I have copied some of my favourite descriptions from the screenplays of some of the most famous films in history, describing the entrances of some of the most famous film characters in history. See if you can guess the characters from their descriptions.

On the landward face of the sail, apparently high in the rigging, is a man for whom the term 'swashbuckling rogue' was coined. – Captain Jack Sparrow from *Pirates of the Caribbean: The Curse of the Black Pearl*

We are tracking in on a fortyish man in Bermuda shorts and sunglasses at the dairy case [in the supermarket]. His rumpled look and relaxed manner suggest a man in whom casualness runs deep. – The Dude from *The Big Lebowski*

He is lounging on his bunk, in white pyjamas, reading an Italian Vogue. He turns, considers her. A face so long out of the sun, it seems almost leached – except for the glittering eyes, and the wet red mouth. He rises smoothly, crossing to stand before her, the gracious host. His voice is cultured, soft. – Dr Hannibal Lecter from *The Silence of the Lambs*

He is in black shirt, black leather jacket. And just enough platinum and diamonds to look like somebody. He reads the paper in a booth. The gun leather-tough LAPD vet is a hands-on, blue-collar cop who can kick your ass with a look. – Detective Sergeant Alonzo Harris from *Training Day*

Impeccably dressed, lean and handsome, he steps out into the lobby like he owns the building – and in a way he does. – Hans Gruber from *Die Hard*

On the surface he appears good looking, even handsome; he has a quiet steady look and a disarming smile which flashes from nowhere, lighting up his whole face. But behind that smile, around his dark eyes, in his gaunt cheeks, one can see the ominous stains caused by a life of private fear, emptiness and loneliness. He is now drifting in and out of the New York City night life, a dark shadow among darker shadows. Not noticed, no reason to be noticed, he is one with his surroundings. – Travis Bickle from *Taxi Driver*

What great descriptions. I'm sure you worked out who each of them was before I told you. It is just as the advice I was given said – hair, clothes and makeup, and how they enter. There are also some brilliant phrases in there to describe some of the characters that mean that no other description is required. I love the phrase "a man for whom the term 'swashbuckling rogue' was coined" for Jack Sparrow. Imagine reading that for the first time as Johnny Depp preparing for the role, or as the costume or hair and makeup departments. The imagination just runs wild. And how about the phrase "a man in whom casualness runs deep" describing The Dude in *The Big Lebowski*? Could Jeff Bridges have played that any more perfectly? And then there's "who can kick your ass with a look" for Alonzo Harris. Any actor seeing that description would bite your hand off to play that character.

Beyond our descriptions, we need to develop our characters throughout our story. How do we do this?

Think about the journey that any character in any story takes and think back to The Hero's Journey. The character learns as they go as they overcome conflict, and by the end of the story they are not the person they were at the start, for better or worse. We have two options for how our audience learns as the story goes. They can either learn at the same time as the character does or they can be one step ahead of the main character (or a combination).

Films with really good twists have the audience learn with the character. Think about the end of *The Usual Suspects* where we learn with Special Agent Dave Kujan as he pieces the whole caper together in his mind whilst staring at the board in his office. Or the end of *The Sixth Sense* when Bruce Willis' wedding ring falls to the floor when he thinks he's talking to his wife and everything comes flooding back to him. Or the ending of *Se7en* when we learn what's in the box at the same time as Brad Pitt's character.

Films where the audience learns before the character (called dramatic irony) include the scene in *The Dark Knight* when Harvey Dent and Rachel Dawes dine with Bruce Wayne and debate with a number of other guests the pros and cons of Batman, little knowing that Batman is sat across the table from them. Or when Simba tries to wake a dead Mufasa in *The Lion King* and Scar tells him to run away in case his mother thinks he did it. The audience knows that Scar killed Mufasa, but Simba doesn't. Or *Romeo and Juliet* where we're told right at the start that the story will end in tragedy and then at the end when we know that Juliet is merely sleeping, but Romeo doesn't, and there's nothing we can do to prevent him from taking his own life.

By learning along with the main character, and sometimes just before, we build empathy for them. We will also build empathy for the character if we see that they are like us. This means that, as much as we hate to admit it, the main character is not perfect. If the main character in your story is the hero, this can be quite difficult. If they're the villain, it may be a little easier. But then we don't want them to be entirely bad either. Our characters need to be believable and relatable. They need to have a mixture of strengths and flaws. If they're heroic, their strengths will outweigh their flaws, and if they are villainous, then their flaws will outweigh their strengths (but don't forget that they will see their flaws as strengths – no villain ever saw themselves as the villain).

It's because of these strengths and flaws that your main character is able to go on the hero's (or villain's) journey. If they were perfect, there would be no refusal of the call, no obstacles to overcome, no death and resurrection. They'd just do it easily, learn nothing, and come home and that would be that. They're going to fail because of their flaws. This is good. Make them suffer, and without embellishing your story too much, push them to their breaking point. Then they're going to triumph because of their strengths.

Despite their flaws, the things that keep the characters going, that keep them pushing on through, are their beliefs, motivations, ambitions and fears. Do you know what they are for your characters? What keeps driving your characters forward through the hell that you're putting them through? These are things that will make your characters unique.

In spite of how the media like to portray the population as divided into two homogeneous extremes, no two people on the planet believe exactly the same things. We might tend in one direction on one issue and in a different direction on another. This means that every individual has a rich tapestry of beliefs different from everybody else's, creating a vast spectrum of thought and opinion across the populous. What does each of your characters believe on the huge array of subjects that are pertinent to your story and beyond? What motivates them? What do they hope to achieve? And what terrifies them (because this can be used to put them through hell)?

It's these beliefs, motivations, ambitions and fears that make our characters interesting.

I've already mentioned that I think *The West Wing* might be the greatest drama ever committed to celluloid. The reason I use the words might be is because whenever I say that, the angel on my other shoulder immediately tells me that I'm wrong, because *The Wire* might also be the greatest drama ever made. I can never decide when I have this argument with myself. In the context of interesting characters though, *The Wire* wins hands down.

You see, in *The West Wing*, all the characters have a very obvious set of beliefs. The president couldn't be a more righteous man, nor could Toby, Sam or Josh, even to the point of self-righteousness in some instances. But in *The Wire*, the line between right and wrong has never been so blurred. The cops and politicians are crooked whilst the gangsters have a clear set of rules and principles that they abide by. Every character is conflicted between what they want to do and what they know they're supposed to do.

The same can be said of *The Boys*, and here it's very obvious. The superheroes, whilst marketed to be the 'good guys' to the world, are on the spectrum of evil whilst the violent, profane, sociopathic gang of superhero killers, led by Billy Butcher, are believe it or not the 'goodies'. It's fantastic entertainment.

This blurring of the lines for the character and the jumbling of beliefs, motivations, ambitions and fears makes for a much more interesting and surprising character than someone who plays it by the book.

When you're telling your story, don't just tell us what the character's beliefs, motivations, ambitions and fears are; demonstrate what they are in your storytelling. Rather than saying, 'Catherine hated cats', you could say something like, 'As the cat arrogantly sauntered across the street without a thought for the lanes of traffic having to slow down around it, Catherine's only thought was how close she could get to it to give it a good scare without hurting it.'

You can also reveal your character beliefs, motivations, ambitions and fears by having the antagonists play against them and show how the protagonist reacts. Through Luke's screams and denial at Darth Vader's speech about ruling the galaxy together in *The Empire Strikes Back*, his beliefs and fears are revealed. Through just his facial expressions during Colonel Kurtz's horrifying speech about the perfect soldier being able to kill without remorse at the end of *Apocalypse Now*, we know Captain Willard's beliefs and ambitions. And as Calvin Candie's lesson in phrenology in *Django Unchained* ramps up the tension, the looks between Dr Schultz and Django, and Dr Schultz's attempts to placate Monsieur Candie, and the anxiety across Django's face and body, all betray their fears and motivations.

While we've talked about your character's motivations and ambitions, it's important to be able to distinguish between your character's wants and their needs. As we discussed in Chapter Two, what your character wants is just that – something they desire because they think it'll make them happy, which then drives them to act. On the other hand, their needs are something more existential. It is what they need to learn in order to overcome their inner demons and achieve true enlightenment, and this is what drives them to succeed. Take *Thor*, for example. Thor wants to become king but needs to learn compassion and humility. In *Toy Story*, Woody wants to be Andy's favourite toy but needs to learn to play nice and work as part of a family. And in *It's a Wonderful*

Life, George wants to escape but needs to remember all the good things that he already has in his life.

The main thing that gives the characters their needs is their past. How well do you know your character's history? What successes and failures have they already had? Who are their parents? What relationships have they had in the past that have made them who they are today? And with this, what baggage do they bring with them that is going to hold them back, or add to the obstacles that you are going to throw at them throughout the story? Again, show, don't tell. Something like, 'This wasn't the first time he'd felt this guilty for walking out on someone,' is far more powerful than, 'and what you need to know at this point of the story is that at the age of twenty-one he walked out on his pregnant girlfriend.'

Their history is also what makes your character unique. No one else has the same history as you, me or anyone else. We all have a unique past. Play on the relevant parts in your story, bring them out, and use the rest to flesh out the character in your mind during the planning so that you know if the character is reacting honestly to the situations and other characters in your story.

This is a lot of stuff to know about each of your characters, all of which will make its way into your story in one way or another, but most of it will never be explicitly said. Like you created an emotion matrix in Chapter Seven, the easiest way to keep on top of each of your characters and to help them evolve as you develop your story is to create a development sheet for each of your characters. The more information that you can put down for each character the better. This will allow you to project well rounded characters rather than two-dimensional caricatures in your story. You can download a character development sheet at www.weareopusmedia.com/ruletheworld.

Success Tasks

- Watch the entrances described in the screenplays above and see how nailed-on the actors' performances are to the descriptions.
- This is a deep one but bear with me. Write down a list of your strengths and weaknesses and how they are linked with your beliefs, motivations, ambitions and fears.
- Watch an episode or two of *The Wire* or *The Boys* to see how the lines between good and bad are blurred and how interesting conflicted characters can be.
- Watch the speeches mentioned above from *The Empire Strikes Back*, *Apocalypse Now* and *Django Unchained*.
- Look back at your emotion matrix from Chapter Seven to refresh your memory on how each of your characters feels at each beat of your story.
- Create a character sheet for each of your characters based on the topics discussed in this chapter.

Chapter 10: Circumstance

"Don't tell me the moon is shining; show me
the glint of light on broken glass"
– Anton Chekhov, playwright

Remember that collective memory thing I mentioned in the previous chapter? About how our subconscious does the hard work for us because of a pool of memories, knowledge and information that we share with people within our social groups? This may be a small social group of friends who were at a particular party with us, or the whole of society who have been educated about a particular event such as the Second World War. Because we think pictorially rather than in words, this collective memory allows our subconscious to fill in the gaps around the information that we take in to complete the picture in our minds. It's a great time saver.

In the same way that collective memory is very helpful when describing our characters, it's very helpful for describing where our story takes place too. There are very few places on the planet that most people have either not experienced or seen in pictures. The same rules apply to describing the setting of the story as to describing your characters. Less is more. Short and sweet and to the point.

To add to this, we want to bring in our five senses to the description. This will engage your audience at every level, allowing them to immerse themselves in the experience and the setting you are describing.

Visual description is the one we naturally use most often.

But let's try and steer away from the obvious primary school descriptions and make our words work hard for us. After all, we've not got many to play with due to the short and sweet rule.

Think about some of the best visuals in film. They don't just display what the director wants us to see; they show us so much more. Think about the shot in *Eternal Sunshine of a Spotless Mind* where Joel and Clementine lie next to each other on the frozen lake staring into the night sky. Next to them in the ice is a giant crack, reminding us of the fragility of their relationship. And do you remember the opening shot of *Citizen Kane*? We see Xanadu, Kane's house, from the imposing gates shrouded in fog, encapsulating Kane's seclusion, separation and sadness. And what about one of the many stunning shots from *The Assassination of Jesse James by the Coward Robert Ford*? Particularly the one where Brad Pitt's Jesse James is silhouetted in the steam on the train tracks by the single light of the locomotive, demonstrating his fearlessness to stare down the oncoming train and how his legend has consumed him, making him all but a shadow to others.

When we're describing locations, we need to be mindful of the above. Let's not just describe the scene as we see it but let's use the visuals to add emotion and character context to the scene. It's ok to describe an object's size, but rather than describing it as big, let's link the character's emotion or personality to its size and describe it as looming. Rather than simply describing a colour as green, let's add meaning by describing the level of colour – is it drab or bright, shamrock green or ulster green? And instead of describing the fog as thick, let's say that the fog kept him secluded from the rest of his family.

By describing the circumstance in which the story takes place in visual terms, you will also connect deeply with those in your audience who are visual learners. Visual learners process, retain and interpret information in visual terms, so by helping them visualise where your story takes place, you will help them engage with your story on a deeper level.

Sound adds extra depth. Have you ever watched a horror film with the sound off? It doesn't work in the same way, if at all. The film by which I have been most frightened wasn't actually a horror film. Although, having said that, the scene from this film is famous for being especially unsettling, and the remainder of the film is a little disorientating to say the least. The film to which I'm referring is *Mulholland Drive* and towards the beginning of the film, there's a scene that takes place in Winkie's Diner in the middle of the day where two men, Dan and Herb, have a conversation about a dream that Dan has had twice before. Dan says that in the dream he sees a man behind the diner with a face that scares him, and that he hopes he never sees the face outside of the dream. Herb suggests that he goes around the back of the diner to see for himself that the man is just in his dream and not real in order to put his mind at ease.

The whole conversation is a very normal dialogue scene with no music and nothing unusual going on. As Dan makes his decision to investigate, the sound of the diner wanes and a dull, monotonous, grinding hum slowly fades in. Everything he described in his dream within the diner begins to happen and his anxiety levels start to rise. Because the sounds of the diner have faded out, the hum starts to become overpowering and distressing, focusing the audience on Dan's anxiety. The two men exit the diner. Dan begins to sweat. He speaks to Herb but we can't really hear what he's saying. Cars whizz by but we don't hear them; the monotonous grind is all-consuming in his head. He's really panicking now. This is just like his dream.

The point-of-view camera focuses on the corner of a wall behind the diner. Dan continues to walk toward it but we can't hear his footsteps, just the monotonous anxiety-inducing hum. He stops and looks at Herb. The hum fades away for a second before he carries on walking and it fades back in. The corner of the wall that he is focused on is getting nearer. He is becoming more and more anxious. His breathing has become faster and faster. Suddenly, a horrifying figure slides out from behind the wall, accompanied by an almighty grinding and shrieking noise. Dan drops to the floor in a state of unconscious terror and the dull, monotonous, grinding hum returns as Herb tries to resuscitate Dan.

This is possibly the greatest jump scare in history. One, because it happens in broad daylight and not in a pitch-black haunted house. Two, because you see the open space where the horrifying figure is going to appear on a number of occasions, so you know it's coming and where it's going to happen, and it still gets you. And three, because of the tension that builds before it. Narratively, it also has nothing to do with the rest of the film and we never see the characters again, though the themes it sets up do resonate throughout.

Having been scared witless by this scene, I was on the edge of my seat for the next two hours of the movie where nothing else remotely scary happens, and I couldn't get to sleep for a good few hours afterwards. I'd have preferred to have watched a horror film with scares throughout because at least that way I would have known what to expect.

Now, why do I tell you this? Because I've watched this scene by itself many times, sometimes with the sound on and sometimes without, and the sound is such a huge part of it. Without it, Dan's initial realisation that he might be about to live his dream doesn't hit home as hard, the build-up of tension isn't the same, and the jump scare isn't really a jump scare. It's just a lady in makeup sliding out from behind a wall. She doesn't actually even jump.

David Lynch, the director of *Mulholland Drive*, really is a master of sound design. His sound tells a story by itself and some of the surreal noises he creates never quite allow a silence in his films to let us have a moment of rest. They keep us in a constant state of unease. You only have to watch and listen to his other films to realise this – the fire sounds throughout *Wild at Heart*, the grinding in *Eraserhead*, and the constant sound of wind in *Twin Peaks*.

Again, by describing the sounds of your story's location, you will engage deeply with those in your audience who are auditory learners. Auditory learners learn through sound and like listening, so by including the sounds of where your story takes place you will connect them to your story on a deeper level.

Have you ever been on one of those 4D experiences at a theme park? For instance, 'It's Tough to Be a Bug!' at Animal Kingdom, 'Terminator 2 3D: Battle Across Time' at Universal Studios in Japan, and the one that scared the life out of me as a teenager, 'ExtraTERRORestrial Alien Encounter' at Magic Kingdom in Florida. If you're not familiar with 4D cinema or a 4D experience, it's when a 3D film is combined with actors and physical effects to bring the whole experience to life.

At the age of fourteen, I visited Magic Kingdom with my family and my dad and I queued to experience 'ExtraTERRORestrial Alien Encounter'. Having enjoyed the pre-show entertainment that Disney are so good at, we were ushered into a theatre in the round. I sat down in a seat and lowered the bars down over my shoulders as if I were about to go on a rollercoaster. On the stage in front of me in the middle of the theatre was a large glass case surrounded by actors dressed as technicians. The show began with two technicians on the monitors explaining that they were on the other side of the galaxy and they were going to teleport one of them to meet the audience. What could possibly go wrong? In their haste to come and meet us, they mixed up their signals, rerouting the teleportation via a distant planet. The next thing you know, instead of the technician appearing in the auditorium, a towering, winged and predatory-looking alien was beamed into the glass case.

As you can imagine, it wasn't pretty. In fact, it was terrifying, particularly to a fourteen year old. The actors in the theatre started to panic and, not surprisingly, the alien escaped the glass tube. To add to the terror, there was a power cut that caused the lights to go out and flicker intermittently. Of course, I was pinned to my seat by the shoulder straps with all this chaos going on and a terrifying alien on the loose. In the dark, a screaming member of the maintenance team ran past me to try and reconnect the power, then I heard a crunch above me and then silence before I felt a gooey liquid drip onto my head. I then heard monstrous footsteps over my left shoulder. As the footsteps got louder, my chair shook with every step until they stopped right behind me. I could feel the creature breathing on the back of my neck and drool dripping from its mouth down my back. Finally, it leapt up, landing on my shoulders and jumping into the tube from where it came, overpowering the electrical supply in the process and exploding goo all over me. My goodness, I could not wait to get out of there.

All the pre-show tension that was built while we waited to enter the theatre helped intensify the terror. The look of the alien added to that. Being in the pitch black certainly didn't help. And the sounds it made and the screams of the actors were very scary. But the thing that terrified me the most and has made this experience live long in my memory is the breath of the alien on the back of my neck. What a genius touch. Whoever came up with that idea needs a pay rise. Hopefully, I don't need to say this, but obviously there was no alien; it was all done with very clever special effects placed in and around my seat. But the effect that this had was to fully immerse me in the experience of believing that there was a hungry alien stood directly behind ready to eat me.

How things feel is such an important part of our place description. Was it hot or cold? Comfortable or uncomfortable? Spacious or claustrophobic? Again, use these descriptions to bring out your character's traits rather than just describe a place. If your antagonist is an imposing character, then perhaps they make the space feel claustrophobic for your hero. If they are a sly snake who is constantly on the move, then maybe they make it feel like the room is in a constant state of revolving. You get the picture.

By describing your circumstance in terms of how it feels, you will also connect deeply with kinaesthetic learners. Kinaesthetic learners learn by feel, touch and by doing, so by describing the place in which your story is set in terms of how they would feel in it, you will connect them to your story on a deeper level.

And how about taste and smell? Think about how you start to salivate when you watch shows like *Parts Unknown*, *Chef's Table* and *Million Pound Menu*. Whether it's Anthony Bourdain enjoying oysters, consommé of oxtail, chilled lobster à la Parisienne and boneless wild hare with fresh black truffle garnish seared directly on a wood stove in a shack on three feet of ice in the middle of the St Lawrence River in Canada, Francis Mallmann cooking lamb al Asador over an open fire in the crisp winter air of Argentina, or Fred Sirieix tucking into a juicy Indian-inspired burger in a pop-up restaurant in Manchester, the suggestion of food, either by sight, smell or statement, causes our brains to react and increase the secretion of saliva.

The same thing happens when we mention taste and smell in our storytelling. Our listeners' brains subconsciously react to the mention of food within the confines of the story by increasing the secretion of saliva, thus engaging them further with the story. And because smell and taste are intrinsically linked – in fact, your sense of smell is responsible for about eighty percent of what you taste – it's important to talk about both the smells and tastes that are apparent at the different locations in your story.

Smell is also the sense that is most strongly tied to our memory. In NLP (neurolinguistic programming), there is a technique called anchoring that involves using an external trigger to elicit a positive internal response. The famous experiment that Pavlov carried out on his dogs, where he rang a bell to elicit salivation in them, is a very good example of this. Jordan Belfort of 'The

Wolf of Wall Street' fame uses this anchoring technique and the fact that out of all our senses, smell is the sense that best triggers memory. Whenever he feels that rush and confidence in closing a deal, he takes a big sniff of a scented essential oil to anchor his high emotional state to that smell. Then, if he's ever feeling low on confidence or needs a boost before a sales meeting or presentation, all he needs to do is take a big sniff of the same oil and the memory of how he felt in that moment of closing immediately returns and instantly saturates his body with confidence.

Our senses are powerful and should be used as such throughout our storytelling. Think about it in evolutionary terms. As the world has changed, who won the evolutionary game? Using all their senses, the ones who responded fastest to the widest range of stimulation and information won hands down.

Having said all this, because less is more and you want to use only one to two sentences, your description of a place may come down to something like this: "As Alex and I entered the noisy station, the air conditioning was a welcome relief, as was the waft of pizza emanating from a nearby restaurant." Simple, huh? You've now got a really good feeling for where I am in the story. It may not be the exact station I'm talking about, but that doesn't matter for my story. Your collective memory has filled in the details. I've started with sound (noisy), then visual (the station and the suggestion that it's busy by saying it's noisy), then touch (air conditioning and suggesting that you've gone from hot to cool), then smell and taste (pizza).

Success Tasks

- The next time you watch a film, keep an eye out for great imagery that means more than just what is in the frame. When you spot something, pause the film and snap a quick picture on your phone to remember it.
- Watch the diner scene from *Mulholland Drive* with the sound on and with the sound off. See and hear the difference that it makes.
- Visit a 4D experience near you.
- Watch an episode of a cookery show of your choice. Pay attention to how your digestive system switches on and how you become more involved in the show because of it.
- Write five short descriptions of where your story takes place using the five senses.

Chapter 11: Context

"Reality is not a function of the event as event, but of
the relationship of that event to past,
and future, events."

– Robert Penn Warren, poet, novelist and literary critic

A story's context brings its characters to life and adds layers to the conflict. Context is anything that tells us more about the characters and why the characters in the story are where they are at that particular moment in time. A lot of the conflict in your story will remain elusive and tenuous without it.

The kind of context that we might want to know includes but is not limited to: the character's family situation, their wealth and financial standing, their social status and expectations, the historical backdrop of the story, the political climate, and any religious or cultural traditions. If you're involved in the story, we may also want to know how you became involved. Did you end up as part of the story accidentally? Did you offer your help? Or are you the cause of the inciting incident that kicked off the whole mess in the first place?

If we didn't understand that Bruce Wayne was a billionaire playboy whose parents were murdered when he was a boy and that he lived in a city overrun with crime, then would we really buy into the character of Batman? A grown man dressed in latex with very expensive toys who runs around the city at night beating up criminals. Probably not. And despite the fact that the whole film takes place in North Africa, the backdrop of the Second World War is essential context for the story of *Casablanca*. Without it, the story simply doesn't work. And what would *Slumdog Millionaire* have been like if it had been set in the UK or the US? The Indian culture and context are fundamental to how that story is told and how it feels.

As you can see, context is essential to the story that you are telling.

Including context in your story also creates points of connection with your audience. When I was growing up, my mum worked five jobs and my dad worked two jobs just to put food on the table and a roof over our heads. Because of this, there weren't many toys in our house so during our play times, my brother Daniel and I would make up stories and play make-believe. This, I believe, is what started me on a path of storytelling and filmmaking. This short story from my childhood is full of context with many points of connection that may land with my audience. The fact that my parents worked hard and had multiple jobs, and that we weren't wealthy, the fact I have a brother, our playing together, and our love of using our imaginations. With just a few sentences, I've created multiple entry points for connecting with my audience by including relevant context in my story, and because I've created these connection points through context, my audience will become more emotionally invested in my story and will be more likely to want to invest further and hear more.

As you can see from the context that I've included in my story, I've not created a huge list or waffled on and on to the point of monotony, but I've used enough details to bring my story and my characters to life and to create a deeper connection with my audience.

Success Tasks

- Next time you watch a film or TV show, write down all the contextual elements that, if they were removed, would mean that the story didn't make sense or would make the characters or situations less engaging. What do you notice about them.
- What connection points can you create in your story by including relevant context?

Chapter 12: Conflict

*"Nothing moves forward in a story
except through conflict."*

– Robert McKee, author, lecturer and story consultant

Without conflict, you don't have a story. It's as simple as that. Conflict is what drives your story by shifting the emotions of your characters from positive to negative and back again in repeating arcs. If there is no conflict, then there is no shift in emotion and therefore nothing to drive the story forward. Think back to the hero's journey. If the hero heeded the call to adventure immediately, continued the journey without encountering any obstacles or enemies, found their treasure without needing to change or fight for it, and returned home without having learnt anything new, then there's not much of a story. It's basically a bloke leaving home, picking something up and coming home again. It's your standard trip to the supermarket, and nobody wants to hear about that unless something out of the ordinary happens en route. There's nothing at stake.

Take *The Silence of the Lambs*. It's a brilliant example of a story full of conflict that has captivated audiences since the book's release in 1988 and the film's subsequent release in 1991.

Let's start by looking at what's at stake for Clarice and the other characters involved in the film. Clarice is a trainee FBI agent who is asked by a very senior officer, Jack Crawford, to interview the psychiatrist, serial killer and cannibal Hannibal Lecter in order to try and catch a new serial killer on the block, Buffalo Bill, who has kidnapped and murdered five women. What's at stake? The lives of Buffalo Bill's next victims. Between Clarice and the FBI team, they have to work hard to capture Bill before he can strike again.

But Clarice's career is also at stake. She sees this as an opportunity to progress by starting in the behavioural science unit where she has always wanted to work. If she does a good job for Crawford, when she graduates from the academy she's sure he'll hire her to his department. If not, will she even graduate at all? Of course, as the story progresses, Hannibal gets inside Clarice's head despite Crawford's warnings not to let this happen. Clarice confronts Buffalo Bill and suddenly what's at risk is Clarice's own life. The stakes are dramatically raised.

When telling your story, you need to do the same. What's at stake for your characters? I would imagine that, more often than not, their life is not in the hands of a cannibalistic serial killer, but who knows? Are they up for a promotion, looking to close the deal of a lifetime or about to get married? And what does life look like for them if everything suddenly falls apart and goes in the opposite direction than they expected? This is a real 'twist the knife' moment. You want to make the audience feel what your character has to lose.

At the climax of *The Silence of the Lambs* when Clarice discovers Buffalo Bill's house and he answers the door, he doesn't just hand himself over admitting to all the crimes he's committed in the process. That wouldn't be a satisfying conclusion to the movie. The filmmakers needed to make the audience squirm, and boy did they. As it dawns on Clarice that she's found Bill, he manages to get away into his basement, which is full of some of the most grotesque imagery ever committed to celluloid. For a good three or four minutes, Bill is nowhere to be found, but we know he's there and so does Clarice. It's only when he cuts the electricity and the basement is thrown into utter darkness that we finally know where he is, with the camera assuming his point of view through the night vision goggles he is wearing as he watches Clarice fumbling around in the dark. He follows her around for a couple of minutes, only millimetres away from her, occasionally reaching to stroke her hair and face. It's only when he finally cocks his revolver to shoot Clarice that she realises where he is and guns him down first, ending the tension once and for all.

What can you do to twist the knife as the filmmakers did at the end of *The Silence of the Lambs*, to make your audience squirm so that they fully appreciate what your characters have to lose?

To help you twist the knife in your audience, it's important to know that, deep down, people are motivated by only two things: the need to remove a pain or the desire to achieve a goal, as we explored in Chapter Six. This is true throughout life, be it removing the risk of getting hurt by refusing to step out of your comfort zone, taking painkillers or sleeping tablets to help you get to sleep, or investing in insurance in case your house floods. On the flip side, setting a savings goal to book that holiday you've always dreamed of, working hard to achieve that promotion, or eating right to hit that weight goal are all examples of goal-orientated motivations.

The vast majority of people are the first of the two, motivated by removing pain rather than by achieving a goal. Once you know how your characters are motivated, you can start to either increase the pain that they are desperately attempting to remove or slowly move the goal posts so that they are constantly just out of reach.

In *The Silence of the Lambs*, Clarice is motivated by both pain and gain. She is motivated to remove the pain inflicted on the women who will become Bill's next victims, and eventually motivated to stay alive rather than die at the hands of Buffalo Bill. The gain that she can achieve is to prove that she has what it takes to outsmart Hannibal, catch Bill, and earn her place in Jack Crawford's team.

What are your characters motivated by? Pain or gain? Or both? How does this reflect what your audience might be motivated by and how can you ensure that it mirrors it? And how, if it doesn't reflect your audience, can you connect them to your character's motivation? In life, most people are more concerned about the potential pain, no matter how small, that they limit their potential and never do the things they could achieve. To add to that, they surround themselves with people who are so risk-averse and concerned about potential pain that they limit them too, ensuring that they never reach the heights they could otherwise achieve.

Once you know what your character is motivated by, it's very easy to throw obstacles in their way to test their motivation and to put them through hell. After all, as I've said, if it's all smooth sailing and there's no conflict, there's no story. In *The Silence of the Lambs*, Clarice is put through all kinds of trials and tribulations as many obstacles are thrown at her, some procedural and some truly horrific. Firstly, Hannibal says no to her request to fill out a questionnaire. A fairly banal obstacle you'd think, but not when the refusal comes from a genius psychiatrist.

Then she comes up against more and more obstacles including Hannibal's fellow inmate's debauchery, Hannibal's trickery and playing both sides against each other, judgement from fellow law enforcement officers for being a woman and for being young, fighting her past, her first autopsy (and not a standard one), and then moving Hannibal from his high security prison to a cage in Memphis, from which he escapes with the potential to track her down and kill her. All of this happens *before* she enters Buffalo Bill's house of horrors, and without going into the graphic detail, the filmmakers throw more obstacles at her in this sequence than in the rest of the film combined. It's a masterpiece in conflict and suspense-building. Real edge-of-your-seat stuff. Who in their right mind would follow Bill down the stairs into that basement?

What obstacles are you throwing in the way of your characters? What are you doing to prevent them from achieving what they want to achieve? If they want to prevent pain, are you twisting the knife and inflicting more and more pain related to what they fear the most? If they want to achieve a goal, are you constantly moving the goal posts so it's always just out of reach? Put your characters through hell, just like Clarice, until the resolution of your story when you can resolve it all and finally give them what they desire.

The other way to add to the conflict is to set something up early and pay it off later. This also adds to curiosity (more on this later in Chapter Nineteen). In *The Silence of the Lambs*, Dr Chilton spends a few minutes mocking Hannibal in his cell while he is strapped to the porter's trolley in his straightjacket awaiting transfer to Memphis. Hannibal notices that Dr Chilton has left his pen on the bed. There's a principle in literature called 'Chekhov's gun' that states that everything we see in a story should be necessary and that, as a storyteller, we should never make false promises; if we talk about a gun in the first act, for example, we should see the gun go off later in the story.

So when the filmmakers show us the pen, we know that Hannibal has a plan. But between that moment and the moment when we see Hannibal take a small piece of metal out of his mouth fashioned from Chilton's pen in the cell in Memphis, fifteen minutes have passed in the film. For fifteen minutes, we've been waiting for something to happen with the pen. For fifteen minutes, we've been wondering what the significance of the filmmakers showing us the pen is, or perhaps we know Hannibal is going to use it for something and, as this scene starts with the wardens bringing food towards the cage, we suspect that the pen is about to come into its own? Of course, Hannibal is then able to use this piece of metal to pick the lock on his handcuffs, release himself, kill the wardens, and escape in the back of an ambulance.

So how are you using the principle of Chekhov's gun to your advantage? What tension are you setting up early on in your story and holding onto, only to use as the payoff later in your story?

Part of the tension that you can build in your story comes down to the type of conflict that you weave into it and into your characters. There are three types of conflict: external conflict, internal conflict and ideological conflict. Let's take a look at each of them in turn using Clarice as our example.

External conflict is what is happening on the outside. Movies where lots of things explode are full of external conflict – *Transformers*, *The Fast and the Furious*, and the majority of the Marvel movies. In *The Silence of the Lambs*, the external conflict is the race against time to solve the murders of the five women to find Buffalo Bill and to save the lives of his future victims. Pretty important stuff. Without it, the film wouldn't have a great deal of tension and pace to it.

In your story, external conflict may be your characters trying to close a sale, striving for promotion, or building their business to a seven-figure turnover.

But if the levels of conflict were left at that, as exciting as the film would be and as exciting as your story would be, there would be less depth. And *The Silence of the Lambs* is full of depth. In fact, the film won the 'Big Five' Oscars and was only the third film in history to do so after *It Happened One Night* and *One Flew Over the Cuckoo's Nest*. The Big Five includes Best Screenplay.

The next level of conflict, internal, is essential. In *The Silence of the Lambs*, Clarice's internal conflict is that, as a rookie agent trying to live up to her sheriff father's good name, she fears that she will fail, and that being put to the test and failing against a genius cannibalistic psychiatrist will show her for who she truly is, who she has been trying to hide since she arrived at the academy – pure white trash. In literary theory, internal conflict is known as 'person versus self'. It's an internal battle that the character must overcome. In *Toy Story*, it's the fact that Buzz Lightyear doesn't realise that he's a toy. In *Fight Club*, the narrator's internal conflict is that he wants to live a more interesting life.

For your characters, they may be attempting to close a sale, striving for promotion, or building their business to a seven-figure turnover because of their search for validation, their self-doubt caused by past failure, or the fact that they don't feel worthy to achieve what they have already achieved. This is the key conflict to excavate in your characters. Your story is likely to have external conflict driving it, but finding the internal conflict will help your characters resonate in the minds of your audience long after they've heard your story.

Think about all the films that win Oscars. Since the start of the twenty-first century, I would class only three Best Picture winners as action films – *Gladiator, The Lord of the Rings: The Return of the King* and *The Hurt Locker*. But these three films include oodles of internal conflict, which is why they won. In fact, the last two both also won Oscars for Best Screenplay, and *Gladiator* was nominated for the award. That must tell you something about how well written they are in terms of conflict. The other Best Picture winners are all dramas that lead with their internal conflict and use their external conflict as a secondary driver.

How about ideological conflict? This really elevates the story head and shoulders above its competition. On the surface, the main ideological conflict in *The Silence of the Lambs* is quite simply good versus evil. In an ideal world, good beats evil and thankfully in this film it does. But the ideological conflict is also elevated by using the Faustian pact that the FBI make with Hannibal to find and capture Buffalo Bill, so that it becomes good *and* evil versus evil. But is this ok? Is it ok to use a cannibalistic serial killer to catch another serial killer? Is it ok to put the not yet fully-trained mind of an FBI cadet in the clutches of a sadistic mastermind to capture another? Once the stakes are raised and a senator's daughter is taken by Bill, is it ok to make a deal with the cannibal to give him new rights if it brings about her safe return and, in the process, potentially endanger others? I don't pretend to be smart enough to know the answers to these questions, but by creating a moral dilemma in the minds of the audience, you once again raise the level of the conflict.

Other films do this very well too. *The Matrix* makes us question our free will. *Snowpiercer* puts classism and power front and centre in the conversation. And any superhero movie raises the question of vigilantism.

In your story, the ideological conflict may be that, as your character has spent more time growing their company, they have spent less time with their children. Or that their work has taken over their life so much that their health has suffered. Or that the next step to growing their company will provide more jobs but will be bad for the environment. These are all ideological conflicts that happen regularly in business. What ideological conflicts do you see in your story?

Of course, understanding who the villain is in your story does help to increase the pressure on each level of conflict. In *The Silence of the Lambs*, there are widely considered to be two villains: Hannibal Lecter and Buffalo Bill. Despite the fact that Hannibal Lecter has topped the charts as the best villain of all time in many polls, looking at the hero's journey, Hannibal walks a fine line between mentor to both Clarice and Buffalo Bill, and therefore plays more of the trickster role with Buffalo Bill as the outright villain. But for the purposes of my next point, let's say that Hannibal is the villain.

One way to increase the conflict whilst also helping the audience to side more with the hero is not to put good sentiment in the mouth of the hero. It often sounds preachy and it's why bad monologues exist. You need to do the opposite. You need to put the argument against the good sentiment in the mouth of the villain. Because remember, the villain doesn't believe that they are the villain. They believe that they are the good guy, doing right in their corner of the world, and often inspiring others to do the same. John Doe in *Se7en* believes his murder spree is justified, even noble, because everyone that he has killed deserved to die as they each committed one of the seven deadly sins, and that he's setting a good example of how to rid the world of 'disgusting people'. In *Misery*, Annie Wilkes is saving her favourite literary character by kidnapping and torturing the author to force him into bringing her back to life. And in *The Silence of the Lambs*, Hannibal Lector's motives for murder are discourtesy, public service and inferiority to himself.

There's a scene in the film where Hannibal is sat in his cell in the dark having had all his drawings taken from him as a punishment for talking the prisoner in the neighbouring cell into suicide for insulting Clarice. Clarice is sat on the floor on the other side of the glass. She asks him about the storage facility that she found based on the clue Hannibal gave her during their previous encounter. In the storage facility, she found a head in a jar. She asks who the head in the jar belongs to. Staying in the shadows to maintain the upper hand, Hannibal responds, "Best thing for him", and lets her know that the head belongs to a former patient that he's tucked away for safekeeping.

He then says, "Just think of him as a kind of experiment." As horrible as this is, it's a brilliant response in terms of putting the anti-sentiment in the mouth of the villain. If the writer had written a monologue where Clarice scolded Hannibal for killing and eating people, and that people deserved to be treated well, Hannibal would have shut her down and it would have broken her character completely. Plus, it wouldn't be believable dialogue because most people don't speak like that. So instead, the writer gave the opposite sentiment to the villain and in just two sentences we are immediately appalled with him. We're more on Clarice's side and we know more about what she's going to have to deal with.

Sometimes though, the villain isn't a person. Sometimes the villain is a situation, particularly in a personal or business context. Think about a financial advisor. In simple terms, they help people to save money for their future. Who's the villain? It's not a person. It could be poor decision making. It could be a lack of financial education. It could be a financial downturn. In all three cases, the financial advisor is there to guide their client to overcome the villain by helping them to make the right decisions, to improve their financial education, and to invest in the best way possible to ride out any dips in market performance. What does that look like for you? How can you put the anti-sentiment in the mouth of a situational villain? It's all about twisting the knife again and making the poor decisions, lack of education and financial downturn as malevolent as possible without over-exaggerating the situation.

Success Tasks

- Watch the trailer for *The Silence of the Lambs*.
- What's at stake for the characters in your story? Write a list of five things for each character and don't stop until you've got five.
- What motivates your character? Pain or gain?
- What obstacles can you throw at your character to

demotivate them and test their mettle?

- What conflict can you set up early in your story and hang onto to increase the tension, in order to pay it off later?
- What are the external and internal conflicts in your story?
- What's the ideological conflict in your story?
- Who's the villain in your story? Why are they the villain? If the villain is a person, what do they believe? If the villain is not a person, what form does the villain take?

Chapter 13: Cure

"I promise you... nobody cares about your
business except for you. Nobody."
– Arvind Gupta, Indian Inventor

We're roughly halfway through the book and have you noticed that we've yet to talk about what *you* do? Have you wondered why that is?

It's because nobody cares about what you do.

Let me say that again in case you think I stuttered as I typed onto the page there.

Nobody cares what you do.

Nor do they particularly care how you do it.

What they *do* care about are the results that you can help them to achieve and the outcomes that you can help them deliver by doing what it is you do. Remember the chapter where we discussed making our clients and team members the hero? That is going to come into play here in a big way. And when I say in a big way, I mean in a big way in principle, because we're hardly going to talk about what it is that we do in our story.

Nobody cares about Gandalf's millennia of studying wizardry and nobody particularly cares that he's a wizard. But when it comes to the crunch, his fellow travellers sure are glad that he put all that time into learning and practising his art so that he could help them cross the bridge at Khazad Dum and the many other times that he helps them to safety. The filmmakers didn't suddenly cut away from the action to a flashback of a young Gandalf sitting in a library at Minas Tirith learning how to be a wizard. Equally, Gandalf didn't turn around to the other characters as the Balrog was about to kill them all and tell them about a list of spells and potions that he could use to destroy it and help them to safety. We only see the very important moments to help keep the story moving along.

For those avid readers of *The Lord of the Rings* who are really interested in the detail, they can delve into the lore of the trilogy in Tolkien's other writings to discover the answers to the questions of where he studied and what spell he used, but for the majority of us, we're happy to move on knowing that the cure that Gandalf presented was to use his expertise to help his friends.

The same can be said for Sean Maguire, Will Hunting's therapist in *Good Will Hunting*. We don't need to see Sean's years of training or even every element of every session that Will has with him. We see the main moments that make a difference and we assume that the rest were the mundane elements of a standard therapy session. And how about Obi Wan Kenobi, or Professor X, or Dumbledore, or Mr Miyagi? Hopefully you get the point I'm trying to make.

Chances are, when you're telling your story, the person you are telling it to already has some concept of what you do, otherwise they wouldn't be talking with you, so there is no need to go into a huge amount of detail about what you do when telling your story. You've already talked about the conflict that your character has faced in your story and you're about to talk about the changes that ensued as a result of the cure that was presented, so just for a moment, you can talk about how you helped your client or team member to overcome it with your cure. Again, notice my phrasing there. How you helped *them* to overcome it. Not how *you* overcame it, because you're the guide and mentor, not the hero.

Let's take an example of a web developer. Web developers these days provide all kinds of services – web design, social media, search engine optimisation, pay-per-click, graphic design, branding, content creation, email marketing – all under the banner of web development. A web developer telling their story could talk about every aspect of their service and how they did this and that, and go into a huge amount of detail. Or, remembering the DISC profile discussion we had earlier, they could simply say that by providing their clients with a combination of web design, social media and PPC, they help them to turn from the conflict (which we talked about in the previous chapter) to the change (which we'll come to in the next chapter). This piques the curiosity of the Ds, does enough for the Is and the Ss because it's shown support, and the Cs (and anyone else for that matter) who want more information on exactly how you achieved the results will ask for the detail at the end of the story.

As I said at the start of the chapter, no one is interested in what you do, so don't waste your time talking about the details and don't bore them to death with them. Tell them what they need to know and move on. What comes before the cure and what comes after the cure are the important bits and the bits that your audience want to know. Hence why this chapter is so short. But don't confuse how short it is with how important it is. When it comes to talking about the cure in your story – what you do – it's like a bank robbery: get in and get out.

Success Tasks

- Look at some brands that you admire. See how few words they use to describe what they do.
- Write down what you do in the fewest number of words you can.
- In your story, what was the cure that took your client or team member from conflict to change? And in how few words can you write this down?

Chapter 14: Change

"Story values are the universal qualities of human experience that may shift from positive to negative, or negative to positive, from one moment to the next."

– Robert McKee, author, lecturer and story consultant

A man relaxes under a mighty oak tree in the middle of a sunny meadow, leaning against a dry stone wall taking some time to read a note left there for him by a friend. The shade takes just enough heat out of the sun without taking away the warmth from the day. He imagines the sound of his friend's voice as he reads the note and smiles. After taking a moment to contemplate his future, he flings his jacket over his shoulder and takes a leisurely walk through the warm and breezy meadow, the scent of wildflowers and the sound of crickets filling the air. He catches a bus, taking a seat at the window allowing the wind to blow on his face, not a care in the world. Having made it to his destination, he walks barefoot on the golden sand of a Pacific Coast beach, once again with his jacket off, his trouser legs rolled up to his knees. The water is every shade of blue, the sun is hot, and the smile on his face is one of contentment, peace and excitement.

Doesn't this sound wonderful? Wouldn't you like to be there right now? I know I certainly would.

You may even recognise what I'm describing. Because, you see, as great as this would be for the majority of us to experience on any given day, this is extra special for the character that I'm describing, because it is not a normal situation that he finds himself in. This is the change that has happened as a result of the cure that has previously taken place. As he says in the voiceover, this is "the excitement only a free man can feel."

What I've recounted here is the last few minutes of *The Shawshank Redemption* as Red makes his journey to find Andy on the Pacific Coast beach after spending forty consecutive years in prison. Can you imagine the feeling of warm sand between your toes and the cool sea breeze on your skin after forty years behind bars? I certainly can't.

It's brilliantly done in the film. The filmmakers show us everything about how his life has changed. Firstly, his circumstances have changed. Everything is expansive. He is never obstructed in the shot by any other object. The field is big, the road is open, the beach is enormous, and even the final shot is from a helicopter as it pulls away to show us the vastness of the ocean. The only time he is inside something – the bus – the window is open. Secondly, his pace of life has changed. He doesn't have to do anything to a schedule or rushed like when he was in prison. All his movements are slow as he meanders through the meadow and saunters down the beach. And thirdly, his mindset and emotions have changed. He's free, he's happy and he has a future, all demonstrated through his body language.

The same goes for you when you're telling your story. You need to describe what's changed in the lives of your characters since the cure was applied. How have their circumstances changed? What emotional shift has taken place? How do your characters look and feel now compared to before?

By being able to answer the question 'what difference have I made for my client?' in these terms you will give your storytelling real impact.

This is often the only thing that will set you apart from your competition - the problems you solve, the outcomes you deliver and the difference you make.

In his book 'What's Your URP?', Andrew Gibson discusses the fact that, nowadays, having a USP doesn't really make you unique. Seemingly everybody has the same USP, which is always focused inwards on you. But what is unique about you is the difference that you make in the lives of your clients, and being able to put that across in a compelling way in your storytelling will be the thing that separates you from your competition.

Take a look back at Chapters Seven and Ten on emotion and circumstances. You need to apply the same principles here but in the context of how the lives of your characters have changed as a result of the cure. How do your characters feel and what do their circumstances look like now? The bigger the difference between before and after the cure, the more impact your story will have, just as Red's story resonates in *The Shawshank Redemption*.

Success Tasks

- Pick a happy defining moment in your life. How have your circumstances changed as a result of that moment? What emotional shift has taken place because of that moment? How do you feel now compared to before?
- Write down ten ways that you make a difference in

the lives of your clients. What problems do you solve? What outcomes do you deliver?

- Re-read Chapters Seven and Ten.
- How have the lives of the characters in your story changed as a result of the cure that was applied, both in terms of circumstance and emotion?

Chapter 15: Carry-Out Message

"And it just goes to show you..."

– Barack Obama, 44th President of the United States

Do you ever listen to someone telling you a story and when they get to the end of it, they just move on with no explanation, leaving you sitting there in bewilderment as to why they told you the story in the first place? It's certainly happened to me on numerous occasions. You sit there wondering what you've just witnessed and will you ever get those few minutes of your life back.

However, when a story is told well, this can be a very effective technique. It comes down to the environment in which you are telling your story, the time your audience has to process it, and the outcome you want to achieve in your audience.

This thinking comes from the world of NLP, or neurolinguistic programming. Telling a story naturally talks to both the conscious and subconscious mind. Of the two, the subconscious mind is the more powerful, so talking to the subconscious mind to elicit a reaction is the preferred option. When we explain the meaning of a story, we break the connection with the subconscious mind and prevent it from interpreting the story on a deeper level and translating it into action.

The technique of telling a story with no explanation works best when we can repeatedly tell similar stories that lead to the same interpretation and action.

A friend of mine, Bill, who is a practitioner of NLP, tells the story of a lady who he was helping through the use of this technique. This lady was suffering from an autoimmune disease.

An autoimmune disease occurs when the body works against itself because its defence system can't distinguish between its own cells and foreign cells. Bill spent three days with this lady in her home in a quiet hilltop village in Italy, telling her stories about how people have worked together for good throughout history, how their teamwork and comradery led to great things, and how their pulling together in the same direction led to history-making moments. Never once did he say why he was telling these stories or explain them to her. He left her subconscious mind to interpret the commonalities between the stories in the hope that it would direct the cells in her body that were misbehaving to work together and start to reverse the disease. And it did. Over the next weeks and months, her symptoms abated, and he gives the credit to the power of her subconscious mind and the power of the many similar stories that he told her. Had he explained each of the stories and broken the connection with her subconscious mind, then in all likelihood, this would not have happened.

The alternative to this, of course, is to tell the audience why you have told them the story, and yes, it will break the connection to the subconscious. But in many circumstances, we don't have three days with our audience in a quiet hilltop village in Italy. Often in a business context, we have less than five minutes to make our pitch as to why someone should buy into our product, service or idea, instead of the next person who is going to try and steal away their attention. This will particularly be the case if you are delivering your story in a place full of distractions.

Think about your past few presentations or pitches. Did you have your audience's full attention? Or was their phone constantly buzzing, or their assistant interrupting, or did the server bring the entrées midway through your pitch? All these interruptions also break the connection with the subconscious mind and prevent it from doing its best work. If you recognise that you're under time pressure, or that the audience you are presenting your story to is busy going from meeting to meeting, or that you are going to be constantly interrupted, then you should absolutely tell them why you have told them the story, and you should make the point succinctly and politely. "The reason I tell you this story is because I believe that we can deliver the same results for you as we did for Joe Bloggs." It's simple, it's to the point, and it gets the message across. It's done just in case the people you are talking to don't quite understand why you have told them your story or haven't got the time to allow their subconscious to interpret it on a deeper level.

Barack Obama delivered many amazing speeches as president. My favourite speech he ever delivered was when he was campaigning for Hilary Clinton in New Hampshire in 2016. It was a story from his campaign trail in 2008 in which he tells us where his famous catchphrase 'Fired up, ready to go' came from. In short, he visited a town in the middle of nowhere in the state of South Carolina on a blustery, rainy day. He was tired having been on the road for weeks, and to make matters worse he got soaked when his umbrella was blown inside out on the way to the venue. As you can imagine, he really wasn't in the mood to deliver yet another stump speech.

Just before he was about to go on stage, he heard a voice from the back of the room shout "fired up" and everybody in the room shouted "fired up". Then the voice said "ready to go" and the crowd responded "ready to go". Obama noticed the woman at the back of the room who had made the initial call that everyone else had joined in with. To say she stood out would be an understatement. Apparently, she was well known wherever she went, and part of her notoriety was for this chant. And because everybody knew her, they knew how to respond. At every meeting she went to, she did this call and response. In this meeting that Obama was at, she kept going with her chanting and the audience kept responding. After a while, Obama started to become fired up and he started to feel like he was ready to go. It changed his whole mood and his memories of the long drive to venue and the fact that he was soaking wet drifted away. The meeting went really well. He got the endorsement of the people there and enjoyed the rest of his day.

It's a fantastic speech that includes everything that I've discussed in this book. After telling his humorous and inspiring story for four and a half minutes, he's built it to a climax. At that point, he pauses and brings the energy down, then begins his carry-out message. He starts by using the phrase "and it just goes to show you…" then continues into why he told the story. As he does so, he builds his energy back up into a real crescendo. Here's his full carry-out message: "And it just goes to show you how one voice can change a room. And if it can change a room, it can change a city. And if it can change a city, it can change a state. And if it can change a state, it can change a nation. And if it can change a nation, it can change the world."

Success Tasks

- Watch Obama's 'Fired up, ready to go' speech.
- Make a note of the locations of all your upcoming meetings and presentations for the next month. Also note how busy the audience is likely to be. Will you have the luxury to allow your stories to hang for your audience's subconscious to interpret the story on a deeper level and take action, or will you need to tell the audience the carry-out message?
- Write three succinct carry-out messages for your story. Until it's well practised, the sentence will probably start, "The reason I tell you this story is…"

Chapter 16: Call to Action

"You can't move people to action unless you first move them with emotion. The heart comes before the head."

- John C. Maxwell, author and speaker

How great is it in movies when the president or the general or the coach calls the people they are leading to action? There are the downright cheesy versions, like in *Independence Day* when President Thomas J Whitmore addresses US fighter pilots at their air force base stood atop a military truck with a loudhailer before sending them off to fight the alien invasion. Or *Pacific Rim* when Marshall Stacker Pentecost (what a name!) stands atop a jaeger and proclaims, "Today, we are cancelling the apocalypse!" There's also the totally inspirational, like in *Gladiator* when Maximus waits on horseback with his troops in a wooded copse to ambush the Germanic horde and rallies his troops with humour, a vision of the future, and the immortal line, "Brothers. What we do in life echoes in eternity." Or there's coach Tony D'Amato's understated speech in the changing room in *Any Given Sunday* where he inspires his American Football team to go out and fight for every inch of the game and be willing to die for each other.

Imagine if these calls to action hadn't taken place. The aliens would have taken over the world in *Independence Day*, the Kaijus would have wiped out humanity in *Pacific Rim*, the Roman soldiers wouldn't have attacked the Barbarians, leading to defeat in the North and perhaps the collapse of the whole Roman Empire, and the Miami Sharks would have failed to come together as a team and would have lost their game.

The same can be said if we fail to call our audience to action after telling them a story. We may have told them the most compelling story, following all the previously laid out rules to give it the best structure and the strongest chance of converting, and we may even have told them the carry-out message so they know why we've told them the story, but none of this is enough if we don't call them to action. If you don't ask, you don't get.

We talked in Chapter Three about beginning with the end in mind and knowing what outcome you want from telling your story. There's no point in going to all the effort of planning and telling an amazing story only to get to the end of it and find that the point you're trying to make is going to lead your audience to take a different action than the one you wanted them to take.

Just as a reminder, your call to action may not be what you first think it is, so really think it through. You may think you want someone to 'buy now' when in fact you really want them to get in touch with you so that you can qualify them first to see if you want to work with them. You may think you want someone to refer you directly to somebody straight away when in fact what you really want is to sit down with the person who is going to refer you so that you can give them more information to help make the referral more successful. You may think you want your team to work harder, but are they working harder at the right tasks or simply working harder on the wrong tasks and burning themselves out?

So it's not just about making sure that we call our audience to action and to the right action, but it's about making sure that we *effectively* call our audience to action. Assuming that you've done ample planning in the 'begin with the end in mind' department, let's look at how you can craft a compelling call to action to add to the end of your story.

Your call to action needs to be clear, and by clear I mean clear in what you're asking them to do, clear in the benefit that they receive, and also clear in how it's phrased. Let me break that down a little bit.

Humans have the capacity to do only one thing at a time, so if you give them more than one instruction, the chances are that they won't do anything. KISS: Keep it simple, stupid. If I ask my toddler Elise to put all her toys away, what tends to happen is that she becomes distracted by the first toy she finds and starts playing with it. So what I do is I help her to put the toys away and name each toy one at a time that I want her to put away and she does it. This is what we need to do with our call to action: use one instruction so that we don't confuse our audience.

The benefit that they will receive if they do the thing that you're asking them to do will have been covered in your story and by your carry-out message, but there's no harm in repeating it here in your call to action. Remember that the benefit that they will receive should be one of the two motivators of people: removal of pain or achievement of a gain. If we simply call our audience to action without reminding them of the benefit, then the chances of them doing the thing we want them to do is greatly reduced than with the benefit attached. If I ask my children to go to bed, the chances of them actually doing it are very slim. I mean, why would they want to do that when being awake is so much more fun? But if I attach a benefit to it and the benefit is one that really motivates them, then you've never seen them move so quickly.

My eldest daughter Alina loves a show on Disney+ called *Brain Games*. It's a short family-orientated show that features interactive games and experiments designed to mess with your mind and reveal the inner-workings of your brain. Though she's only six, it's her favourite thing to watch with me. If I ask her to go to bed under normal circumstances, it can take half an hour to get her there on a good night. But on the odd occasion when I've said that she can watch an episode of *Brain Games* before bed, I've said that she has to go to bed early and take no more than five minutes to get ready. Like magic, as soon as my benefit-led call to action leaves my mouth, the rest of bedtime seemingly takes care of itself with no prompting from me. She immediately stops what she's doing, runs upstairs, gets ready and is in bed within less than five minutes. The key though is to keep the call to action short, to the point and, as we've discussed before, to go easy on the adjectives. You don't want to sound manipulative after all the hard work that you've put in up to this point.

Which leads me on to your wording. It needs to be clear and precise, leaving your audience in no doubt what you're asking of them. Using verbs instead of adjectives will more likely move your audience to action, particularly if the verb is a commanding word such as build, grow or join. These types of words also provoke enthusiasm and tie nicely back into the benefit that your audience will receive from you. You can also add in words that provide hope of the benefits that you are going to deliver, such as results, guarantee and save.

We've discussed motivating people by describing the achievement of a goal and by talking about the benefits that you can deliver in your call to action, but you can also add in a 'fear of missing out' (FOMO) to motivate those who are driven by the removal of pain. This will tap into a number of human emotions in your audience including panic, greed, comparison, curiosity and pride. Using words and phrases like urgent, deadline and limited supply will induce all these emotions in your audience and push them towards buying into your product, service or idea.

With these ideas in mind, let's take a look at a real-life example of a great call to action.

CVS ran an online advert for their stores with the call to action, "Unlock extra savings with app-only deals." Does it have one desired outcome? Tick. Clear benefit? Tick. Clear phrasing? Tick. Short and to the point? Tick. Starts with an action verb? Tick. Provokes enthusiasm? Tick. Provides hope? Tick. Creates FOMO ("app-only")? Tick. Wow. How good is that?

What does your call to action look like at the end of your story?

Success Tasks

- Write three calls to action that include all the principles that we've discussed and A/B test them over your next fifteen presentations to see which gives you better results.

Chapter 17: Conversation

"Dialogue is a lean language in
which every word counts."
– Sol Stein, author and publisher

We've now covered the main structural elements of your story, but we're not done yet. There are still things that need adding in to flesh out your story further to make it more emotionally engaging.

The first of these is conversation or dialogue.

If you were writing a play or a television script, dialogue would be a major part of your story, a little less so for a film script or novel. But for a sales story, dialogue can have a major impact by being used very sparingly and for this reason you need to plan your use of dialogue carefully.

Dialogue should be inserted at the most emotional moments of your story to emphasise them by breaking up the narrative and giving a jolt to your audience. If you were to have dialogue run throughout your story it would lose its emphasis and become more expositional rather than being a tool to develop your characters and their relationships and to move the story along.

The reason that dialogue works at the most emotive points in the story is because, as we've discussed, your story is about the people involved and how they react to the events taking place rather than the events themselves. It's the change in the emotions of the people that is driving the story. Highlighting them with dialogue brings extra gravitas and depth to these already poignant moments and serves to exaggerate the emotional highs and lows of the story.

When using dialogue to add to the weight of the emotional moments in your story, describe the emotional impact of what was said on the characters it was said to and sometimes even on the person who said it.

Once you know who was involved and what was said, it's important that your dialogue doesn't become a tedious, "he said, and then she said, and then he said, and then she said," back and forth. Pinpoint the crux of the conversation that caused the swing in the emotion; it was probably only one or two sentences in reality. Admittedly, there will have been the build up to it and the fallout from it, but when you give it some serious thought, and this is the case in any argument or fall out, marriage proposal or business proposition, there will be that one key line of dialogue that really swung the relationship – "You're not good enough", "I hate you", "Will you marry me?", "Let's do business". This is the exact line of dialogue that you should focus on at each emotional moment that you want to emphasise.

But how do you write good dialogue? Let's take a look.

The rule of any good dialogue is that it must serve a purpose. This purpose is to develop the characters and their relationships or to drive the story forward, preferably both. I used the word expositional earlier in the chapter. Exposition is the opposite of developing the character, their relationships, or moving the story forward. Expositional dialogue is giving information that you could give in the narrative of the story and is a waste of your dialogue. Complex sci-fi movies often have no choice but to use exposition in their dialogue to explain the world in which their movie is set but often do it in an entertaining way. *The Matrix* and *Terminator* both use chase scene dialogue to embed their exposition. We don't need to do that because what we're describing can be a part of our narrative description. Save your dialogue for the real emotional stuff.

To drive our story forward is to change the direction of the story, either in a big way at one of our turning points or in a smaller but still significant way by revealing a pertinent piece of information. This is why it works so well at our emotional moments.

To reveal our characters, we need to know who our characters are. Thankfully, you should already know this from the character exercises that you've done in Chapter Nine. If you know your characters, you will know how they sound when they speak. Every character in your story should sound different to the point where if you wrote down a line of dialogue for each of them, anyone reading the line would be able to tell the difference and know which line of dialogue belonged to which character.

Consider a character like Juno from the movie of the same name. She is a unique character but if she sounded like every character that you've seen in every other movie, she would certainly be less unique. She has her own way of speaking. Or how about the characters that the Coen Brothers or Quentin Tarantino write? Take *The Big Lebowski*. A line from The Dude is clearly distinguishable from a line delivered by Walter, Donnie or The Jesus. And in *Pulp Fiction*, Jules and Vincent are clearly distinct individuals even on the page, just from the way they talk. The important thing about Juno, The Dude and Jules is that the way they speak throughout each movie is consistent, and it should be the same for your characters. If they use big words to demonstrate their intelligence when simpler words would suffice, then they should do this every time they speak throughout your story. If they're abrupt or curse or speak kindly, then this is how they should talk every time they talk.

The way your characters speak to each other will also demonstrate their relationships. Yes, someone who curses will usually curse in conversation, but in front of their loving mother they will likely tone it down, compared to someone who they passionately dislike where they will likely let loose with all manner of expletives. Think Joe Pesci's character Tommy DeVito in *Goodfellas*.

When describing how someone speaks, try to develop your vocabulary past 'said'. Jerome Stern, who was for many years the head of the English Department's creative writing program at Florida State University, stated in his book 'Making Shapely Fiction' that, "Dialogue is not just quotation. It is grimaces, pauses, adjustments of blouse buttons, doodles on a napkin, and crossings of legs." With that in mind, how did your character deliver their dialogue? Did they whisper? Did they announce? Did they pontificate? Did they shuffle on the spot before delivering it? This gives you a better understanding of the character and their relationship with the people that they are in conversation with. Someone who hisses their dialogue at someone clearly has less respect for them than someone who reassures them.

You can also talk about the body language of the person when they are talking. Posture, eye contact, mannerisms and reactions all add to the depth of the character and their relationships. By describing how someone speaks, you are also demonstrating how they feel rather than having them explain how they feel. Show, don't tell. Having a character say, "I'm sad to tell you that Grandma has died," is not only a wasted half-line of dialogue but could so easily pack more of a punch by describing body language and how they delivered the line, and by cutting the line in half. Try, "Mum stood at the door. I could see that something was wrong. She couldn't get her words out. But when she did, all that she could manage was, 'Grandma's gone'."

Your lines of dialogue should be short. "Grandma's gone" is far more powerful than any monologue that could have been said in its place. Plus, a long monologue will cause your audience to get lost between the character speaking and the narrative, especially if you are delivering your story verbally. To help with this, and the rule about moving the story, characters and relationships forward, there's no need for small talk and greetings in your dialogue. I bet that once you've written your dialogue down you can probably remove the first word, if not the second and third, and the sentence will still make sense. Keep it snappy and it will add to the emotional punch.

Finally, once you have written your dialogue down having followed the guidelines outlined in this chapter, say it out loud to see how it flows off the tongue. Dialogue doesn't have to be entirely natural. After all, the words and phrases that Juno speaks or most of the characters in the Coen brothers' films aren't entirely natural – they would certainly stand out a mile if I met them at my local supermarket – but the dialogue that they deliver does flow nicely off the tongue of the actors portraying the characters. The same needs to happen with your dialogue. Does it have rhythm and cadence, or is there a word that trips you up when you say it out loud? It's a good idea to check these things before adding them back into your story at the most poignant moments.

Success Tasks

- Pinpoint the emotional high and low points in your story. Who is involved? What conversations took place between these people? What one or two lines of dialogue were the most important in this conversation?
- Check that your dialogue serves one of the three purposes that we have discussed – moves the story forward, shows character or builds relationships.
- Write down this famous line of movie dialogue from *On the Waterfront* as said by each of your characters, ensuring that it is distinct for each of their voices: "You don't understand! I could've had class. I could've been a contender. I could've been somebody, instead of a bum, which is what I am."
- How do your characters speak their lines of dialogue? Whisper? Announce? Pontificate? Or something else? And what are their posture, eye contact, mannerisms, reactions and emotions like when they're talking and being spoken to?
- Write down any dialogue that you have chosen to include in your story and make sure that it has a unique voice.
- Remove the first few words from each line of dialogue until it doesn't make sense anymore.
- Read your dialogue out loud and amend it so that it

flows smoothly off your tongue.

Chapter 18: Comedy

"Laughter connects you with people. It's almost impossible to maintain any kind of distance or any sense of social hierarchy when you're just howling with laughter. Laughter is a force for democracy."

– John Cleese, actor, comedian, screenwriter, and producer

What's the funniest movie you've ever seen? Or what scene in a movie has you doubled up every time? Or who's the greatest stand-up comedian ever?

It's funny isn't it that everyone will have a different opinion on this. Every list of the funniest films of all time has different films in the top ten. I think if I were to combine five or six of the lists I could create a top ten that I agree with. Every list of the funniest movie scenes of all time tends to agree, and I disagree with almost all of them. And every list of the greatest comedians of all time contains about fifty percent who I think are brilliant and fifty percent who I think don't belong amongst the greats.

Comedy is a matter of taste because of the sheer number of genres within comedy and what different people find funny. For example, I love absurdist comedy, so Monty Python, *Anchorman* and Eddie Izzard make me laugh every time I watch them. I also enjoy dark comedy, so *Family Guy*, *Three Billboards Outside Ebbing, Missouri* and Dave Chappelle are right up my street. But I don't appreciate crude humour as much as some people do, so *South Park*, *Bridesmaids* and Amy Schumer don't float my boat, despite how good at it they are. The thing about all great comedy is that, within its genre, each example will follow a series of principles that creates the humour, which we'll take a look at shortly.

But before we do, why do you think that comedy in storytelling, particularly when we're attempting to sell a product, service or idea, is important? In his book 'The Sales Bible: The Ultimate Sales Resource', Jeffrey Gitomer says, "If I can get the prospect or customer to laugh, I can get him or her to buy." It's because humour is the best tool to build rapport with. It's humanising and a bit of a leveller that allows you to quickly find common ground. Humour also puts people at ease (so long as it's the right type of humour. More on this later). It breaks the tension in what can sometimes be an awkward situation. It may be the first time you've met someone or they've seen you deliver, so it shows them that you're likeable, intelligent, and that you are approachable. It increases coopetition because laughter is contagious. It stimulates the parts of the brain responsible for memorising information, making you more memorable, and the parts of the brain responsible for reducing stress, lowering blood pressure, improving alertness and increasing creativity. And it will help you stand out from the crowd. So, the earlier in your story that you can get your audience to laugh, the better.

As we discussed in Chapter Seven on emotion, adding levity into your story, particularly if there are more serious elements to it, also helps to swing the emotions of your story, making it more engaging. Remember the stories from *Scrubs* about the Ken Griffey Jr baseball card or from *The West Wing* about Mrs Landingham going to the funeral?

As president of the United States, Barack Obama was known

for many things: being a great leader, sticking to his convictions, perseverance, energy, bringing about change, taking risks, and being a great communicator. Part of his being a great communicator was his ability to add humour to his communication at the right moments and to not take himself too seriously.

As we've mentioned before, Obama delivered many great speeches. Some were outright hilarious, such as when Keegan Michael Key became his 'anger translator' Luther at the White House Correspondents' Dinner where he aggressively interpreted the president's inner anger while the 'mellow' president calmly addressed the audience. How Obama kept a straight face I have no idea. Others were heartfelt and demanded no humour whatsoever, such as in his eulogy for the Honourable Reverend Clementa Pinckney in the aftermath of the tragic shooting at the Charleston Church massacre.

My favourite speech ever delivered by Obama is a speech that we've already talked about in Chapter Fifteen where he retells a story from his campaign trail in 2008 about his famous catchphrase, 'Fired up, ready to go'. Although it is an inspiring story rather than a funny one, his use of humour elevates it to the next level. The jokes aren't jokes per se. There's no opening knock-knock joke and it's never raucous like a Dave Chappelle set, but the whole story is light and breezy. The humour is observational and self-deprecating, and the attention to detail is enough to paint a whimsical picture.

The thing I notice when watching (other than the audience laughing at the right moments and everyone in camera shot smiling) is that every time I do, I smile all the way through too. It's like a piece of music with a rhythm that you can't help but tap your foot to. This is the kind of humour that manages to raise a smile on everyone's face. Then when the president hits you with his carry-out message it catches you off-guard, because the tone shifts to super energetic and super inspiring and you can't help but be carried off with it. It's so well written, so well delivered, and so effective.

With all this in mind, what does good comedy look like and how can you implement it into your storytelling?

Comedy is the meeting of two ideas that don't match. It's the element of surprise and unpredictability. It's subverted expectations. Let's start off by looking at a very simple joke to see how this works.

The semi-lovable misanthrope WC Fields is famous for the following joke way back in 1941: "I was in love with a beautiful blonde once. She drove me to drink. That's the one thing I'm so indebted to her for." Do you see what he did there? The ideas don't match and the punchline comes out of left field – the basis for all comedy.

Take the newscaster brawl in *Anchorman* where Ron and his team are out for a stroll to buy new suits, only for the other news teams to appear out of nowhere, for no good reason, pulling all manner of insane weapons from inside their suit pockets. In a matter of seconds, it's a full-on *Braveheart*-style fight scene with horses, people on fire, pitchforks and severed limbs in the middle of downtown San Diego. "Boy, that escalated quickly."

Or how about the food poisoning scene in *Bridesmaids*? The ladies are trying on bridesmaid dresses in a very upscale bridal boutique when the food poisoning starts to set in. Seeing beautiful ladies in gorgeous wedding dresses going through the various violent bodily expulsions for the next few minutes certainly ticks the boxes of mismatched ideas, the element of surprise and subverted expectations. And what about the Black Knight in *Monty Python and the Holy Grail*? The Black Knight's calm reaction to losing his arm – "'Tis but a scratch" – and his continued determination to fight and defeat King Arthur despite losing the rest of his limbs certainly demonstrates the underlying principles of comedy outlined here.

As with all three of the examples given, many comedic scenarios allow the conflict and jeopardy to build and build until you think it can't possibly get any worse, then somehow it does. In the aforementioned scene in *Monty Python and the Holy Grail*, the Black Knight first loses his left arm, at which point in a normal scenario any individual would seek life or death medical attention, and in the medieval times in which the film is set he would have likely died. Yet in this scene, he doesn't flinch and in fact continues to fight, losing his right arm next and fighting on by attempting to kick King Arthur to death, calling it "just a flesh wound" before having both legs chopped off. Even when he's just a head and torso on the ground, he still wants to fight, calling the contest a draw and threatening to bite King Arthur's legs off. It's a great example of escalation.

You can see how far you can escalate the humour in your story by using the rule of thumb in improvisational comedy called 'Yes, and...' The idea is that during the improv, the actor accepts what their counterpart has said or done (yes) and then expands on their line of thinking (and...) in order to keep the flow of the performance going and expand the world of the show. You can do the same with the comedic elements of your story to bring more humour to it. Instead of stopping where the humour has ended, say to yourself, 'Yes, and...' then develop the humour further. 'Yes' I accept where the comedy has taken me this far 'and' I am going to take it further. By building on the humour like this, you can add more layers of comedy into your story to swing it to new heights of emotion, help it to resonate further, and to stay with your audience for longer.

It is, however, important to know when to stop. The only way of knowing this will be to test it on a few audiences. My suggestion is to push it past the point where you are comfortable and then test it on some people that you really trust. This is what stand-up comics do. They have safe test audiences (family and close friends) and then they try out their material at test gigs in front of smaller audiences, where their phones are locked away and no journalists are allowed in, to see how the material is received.

As you will have noticed in the examples above, the way that the humour often occurs in storytelling is because something flies in from left field just when things are going well. Remember, unpredictability is fun. In *The Big Lebowski*, The Dude lives a happy life, generally lazing about being a cool dude, bowling with his buddies and keeping himself to himself. That is until one evening when he comes home from buying milk to find two men in his house. He is immediately tackled by one of them and dragged into the bathroom before having his head shoved down the toilet. After a moment, the thug holding his head in the toilet gives him a reprieve, pulls his head out and demands "Where's the money, Lebowski?" before immediately slamming his head back down the toilet without giving him any time to respond.

This pattern continues a few more times before the thug throws

The Dude from the toilet and gives him a little more context, and thug number two starts to urinate on the rug in the lounge. It is immediately apparent that they've got the wrong guy and the mix up is because he shares a surname with the man they're after. This sets up the rest of the movie as The Dude attempts to have his rug replaced by the man that the thugs have confused him with and, as a result, he becomes embroiled in a kidnapping plot. In my world, having your head used as a toilet brush and someone urinating on your rug is definitely out of left field, especially when you're on your way back from the grocery store, but it certainly sets up a whole heap of hilarity throughout the rest of the film.

Mel Brooks of *Young Frankenstein* and *The Producers* fame once said that the essences of humour are anticipation and payoff. This is essentially your standard joke structure taken to the next level. You set the joke up and then you deliver the punchline, but with anticipation added into the middle, so it becomes setup, anticipation and payoff. The setup is important because without it you don't have any context. The payoff is important because that's where you get the laugh. The anticipation is where you can enhance the reaction by drawing out the story, postponing the punchline, and withholding as much necessary information as possible to keep your audience on the edge of their seats knowing that something is coming, but not what is coming and when. During this anticipation stage of your story, you can throw in jab-lines. They're not as much of a knockout as a punchline, but they're funny quips, little funny jabs that keep your audience smiling and laughing as you build up to your big payoff.

For me, call-backs are one of the most underappreciated weapons in the comedy arsenal. Call-backs are when a comedian tells a joke and delivers a punchline then later on in the set, the comedian tells a different joke and delivers the same punchline. Call-backs work because they take the audience by surprise again and double down on the original joke. It's kind of like an inside joke between the comedian and the audience. It makes the audience feel special, giving them a sense of familiarity and creating further rapport. Dave Chappelle is the king of the call-back. Six of his seven hour-long specials end with a call-back, as well as sprinkling them throughout the rest of his sets. Eddie Izzard uses call-backs throughout all her sets too, even repeating an entire sequence in French, relying on the audience understanding the jokes that she previously said in English. And for any *Family Guy* fans out there, there's the recurring joke of a giant chicken showing up and fighting Peter for five minutes of the episode despite it having nothing to do with the storyline. If you can do the same in your story by calling back humorous elements from earlier on, then you will double down on your comedy and create an inside joke with your audience.

When implementing humour in your story, it's important to analyse two things: your audience and your style of humour.

Firstly, by analysing your audience you will know how appropriate it is to incorporate various genres of humour. The majority of talks that I have delivered have been at professional business conferences, so the humour in my stories has always been gentle and appropriate. However, I have also delivered best man speeches and after dinner speeches at various societies where a certain level of humour is expected. If you get this mixed up, then you will find that your stories will not go down well and you will not get invited back. Even in my best man speeches, I am always aware that there are likely to be grandparents and possibly children present at the wedding breakfast, so even though the stories may be outrageous and the humour in the style of a roast, my language is always appropriate and I know where to draw the line, and when to use innuendo and not be explicit.

Secondly, by analysing your own style of humour, you will know what will work for you and what won't when you are telling your story to your audience. For example, for the life of me I can't remember a joke. Not one. So, any kind of humour that is going to require me to remember a particular phrase or word is not going to work for me. But I have been known to be sarcastic. So acerbically stating the obvious, being ironic, or using understatement to bring humour into my stories works well for me.

What is it for you? Are you good with word play like George Carlin? I love George Carlin's quote, "Think of how stupid the average person is and realize half of them are stupider than that." Or, like John Oliver, can you make brilliant and funny analogies? Such as, "New Year's Eve is like the death of a pet. You know it's going to happen, but somehow you're never quite really prepared for how truly awful it is."

Are you the master of the deadpan like Steven Wright, who can state the obvious and make it funny without cracking so much as a smile? I love his deadpan delivery of, "It's a good job there's gravity otherwise when birds died, they'd just stay right up there." Or can you deliberately misread situations and play dumb like Peter Kay in his brilliant routine about misheard song lyrics? Are you a great observer of everyday life like Jerry Seinfeld?

Are you larger than life like Tracy Morgan? Are you ironic like Steve Martin? Or sarcastic and good at the understatement like Bill Hicks? Or cantankerous like Bill Burr? Or self-deprecating like John Mulaney? The list goes on and on... absurd, farcical, highbrow, physical, and so on.

What natural style or styles of humour can you employ in your storytelling? Which can you learn? Which, for the time being at least, should you avoid? Don't try to be funny in a style of humour that doesn't suit you. It won't work and you'll come off looking obnoxious and unfunny.

Once you know which style you are suited to, you can work to enhance it by finding comedians that match your style and studying them. See how they write their jokes and material. See how they setup their jokes, how they build anticipation and add in jab-lines, and how they deliver their payoff. Watch their material and pick your favourite moments. Write it out so you can really analyse it. Learn a few minutes of it and practise delivering it out loud. This is how many of the greatest stand-ups of all time have done it.

By doing this and then practising your own stories with humour in, you will improve the delivery, pace and timing of your jab-lines and punchlines. Comic timing and rhythm are essential. I'm sure we all know someone with a great sense of humour on the page, but with the worst sense of comic timing when it comes to their delivery. Do you remember the scene in the first *Borat* documentary when Borat visits the humour coach to learn about comic timing? The humour coach teaches Borat the simple premise using a 'not' joke.

In the film, Borat is wearing a grey suit, so the humour coach says, "This suit is black... that's a pause... not!" I'm sure we can all agree that this is not a very good joke but, sticking with the principle of comic timing that he's trying to demonstrate, Borat then goes on to butcher the joke time and time again by getting his timing and rhythm totally wrong, thus proving the point that the pause in the middle is essential for the joke and that timing in comedy is crucial. The pause in this joke is called a pregnant pause, a second or two of silence to create an expectation in the audience before subverting their expectation. Comic delivery can also include slowing down and speeding up the tempo of your delivery and can even include changing the volume at which you deliver your story.

When you listen to any top-notch comedian delivering their stand-up, you will also notice how varied their vocabulary is. This enables them to not only keep you engaged but to describe things in entertaining and specific ways. I love Eddie Izzard for this. Not only can she deliver her stand-up fluently in four different languages, but her grasp of the English language is outstanding. It's no wonder that John Cleese called her the "lost Python". It's important that you develop your vocabulary in your storytelling too, particularly when it comes to the humorous elements. It will allow you to describe things in a detailed and heightened way to truly demonstrate that the ideas you are putting forward don't match.

Just a few more pointers to help you to find the funny. Generally, just try and relax and take life with a pinch of salt. If you take everything seriously then you will never see the funny side of things, and as Natalie Portman's character Sam says in *Garden State*, "If you can't laugh at yourself, life is going to seem a whole lot longer than you'd like." Pay attention to the world around you. Funny stuff is happening all the time. And even when it isn't, say for example when something happens in life that wasn't as you had planned it, try and find humour in it and analyse it for its absurdity and comic value. The old adage that 'comedy is tragedy plus time' is true for a reason.

Here are a few things to avoid in your storytelling humour in any selling situation. Don't make jokes at someone else's expense, which includes stereotypes, the competition, and the person or people you're talking to. Being mean will just make you look bitter, uninformed or, at worst, bigoted. There's also no room for coarseness or crudeness. It will make you seem unprofessional. Don't recycle jokes that someone may have heard elsewhere as this will make you seem unoriginal, but the usual rule of 'don't discuss politics, religion and money' in your humour doesn't necessarily apply. This will all come down to knowing your audience, as we discussed earlier. It may be a big mistake to talk about these topics, but at the same time, if you are telling your story to persuade your congregation during your sermon, then religion is obviously a necessary topic, as is politics if you're delivering a campaign speech, or money during a sales pitch. I'll leave these finer details to your discretion.

Success Tasks

- If you haven't already watched the 'Fired up, ready to go' speech by Barack Obama, go and watch it.
- Buy a 'word of the day' calendar or subscribe to a

word of the day email to improve your vocabulary.

- Analyse your style of humour. What style (or styles) do you have? What styles don't you have? Watch a stand-up special from a comedian with a similar style to you and analyse how what they deliver works.
- Go and sit in a busy place and observe what is happening for an hour. Take a notebook and write down as much as you can about the people you see (conversations, interactions, what they do, etc.). Once you get home, go back through your notes and highlight anything that stands out as funny, fundamental to the human experience, or which connects with you on a personal level. Pick one idea and write ten jokes from it using the setup, anticipation and punchline formula. They don't have to be good. Just write them. Don't stop until you have ten.
- Carry out the 'Yes, and' exercise to the humour in your story.
- Practise the jokes in your story out loud to your closest family and friends, or to a small focus group.
- Decide which elements of your story can work as a call-back.
- Analyse your audience for your next five meetings. What elements of humour will be appropriate?

Chapter 19: Curiosity

"There is only one plot – things
are not what they seem."

– Jim Thompson, author and screenwriter

The most important element to a story is to make the audience want to know what happens next. I can't stress this enough. It's true that without conflict there is no story, but if the audience don't care what happens next, if you've not piqued their curiosity, then why would they stay invested and continue to pay attention until the end?

My wife and I watched a film recently that was written and directed by an Oscar-winning director, starred a pair of two-time Oscar-winning actors, another Oscar-nominated actor, and a Golden Globe-nominated actor. Despite all this, we simply didn't care what happened next. Needless to say, we didn't particularly enjoy the film, and there are many examples of films just like this. Some of these films will be loud, flashy, big-budget action films that despite all their bravado can't keep the attention of their audience. Sometimes a small, thoughtful, low-budget drama can keep an audience on the edge of their seats all the way through by simply ensuring that they want to know what happens next.

Do the Right Thing is a great example of a low-budget drama that keeps the audience's attention from the very beginning until the very end. From the moment the alarm clock rings in a close up on a clock with the time at 8am and Samuel L Jackson's radio announcer, Mister Señor Love Daddy, starts with his, "wake up, wake up, wake up, wake up", you want to know what's happening.

What's the significance of 8am? As the camera pulls out and we start to see the radio studio and Mister Señor Love Daddy announces that the weather is hot, and that black is the colour of the day, and we get a glimpse of outside as the street starts to wake up, we want to know why the information that we've just been given is relevant. Every sentence he utters really is pertinent information.

As the drama unfolds, the whole film taking place on the hottest day of the year on a street in Brooklyn, we get to know each of the characters. Every interaction leaves us wondering what is going to happen next. Every decision that each character makes leaves us asking a question as we watch their hate and bigotry smoulder and escalate until it explodes into violence. Even at the end of the film, the question I was left with was, 'what will happen next in each of the character's lives?' What a brilliant way to end a film. The main story arc is resolved but the larger moral dilemma raised is well and truly brought to light, and the film doesn't let us off easily.

How about great TV shows? I remember watching *The Wire* for the first time; every episode would end leaving me with the feeling of wanting more. I watched all five series of *The Wire* in five weeks – that's sixty episodes – because of the curiosity that it generated in me. When that brilliant piece of music by Blake Leyh in the end credits kicked in, it created an almost Pavlovian response, and I had to put the next episode on. It had me hooked. I was exhausted in work for those five weeks because it didn't matter how early I put the show on, I would always need to watch just one more episode way too late into the night, and not necessarily because it always ended on a cliff-hanger. It was just compelling television.

Dexter, on the other hand, always ends on a cliff-hanger. There were no early nights as I worked my way through those boxsets either. But I learnt my lesson. When the first season of *Stranger Things* debuted on Netflix and I became immediately hooked, I took a day off work to complete the series so that I wasn't exhausted by sitting up late at night watching 'just one more episode'. By then, I had children and couldn't afford to miss out on my much-needed sleep.

Speaking of Netflix, in February 2017, Wired magazine published some data in graphical form from Netflix that showed the length of some of their most popular series in minutes, broken down into episode chunks. Highlighted was an episode that they called the 'hooked episode'. The hooked episode is the episode after which seventy percent of the audience completed watching the entire series. For Marvel's *Jessica Jones*, it was episode four, for *House of Cards* it was episode three, and for *Breaking Bad* it was episode two. I'd love to know what moment it was in those episodes that made seventy percent of the audience say to themselves that they were in it to the end. This shows the value of grabbing attention at the start of your story as we discussed in Chapter Four and ensuring that there is enough curiosity generated in the early stages so that it's not all left to the end for the climax.

Before the advent of Netflix, and still to this day, network TV shows have had to build curiosity into each episode because of commercial breaks to make sure that the audience returns after the ad break is over. The writers have to leave mini cliff-hangers every ten to twelve minutes so that the audience are engaged enough in the story and want to know what happens next, enough to be able to sit through a commercial break or to go and make a cup of tea and come back to find out the resolution. But this is nothing new. Since the serialisation of Charles Dickens' stories, cliff-hangers have been part of our culture, leaving his readers sitting up at night saying to themselves, 'just one more chapter.'

But what do *Breaking Bad*, *The Wire* and *Do the Right Thing* all have in common? And what tools do they, like all good storytelling, employ to generate curiosity to make the audience want to know what happens next?

The answer is that they all create a curiosity gap. The term 'curiosity gap' is based on the information gap theory of curiosity by Carnegie Mellon University Economics and Psychology professor George Lowenstein. It refers to the psychological effect created when someone is aware of a gap between what they know and what they don't know and is motivated to resolve it. It's stating the obvious to suggest that curiosity is essential to intrinsically motivated learning. After all, it's how we all learn and have learnt since we came into the world. All good storytelling leans heavily on our human desire to want to close the curiosity gap.

Let's take a look at the elements in storytelling that help to create a curiosity gap.

In the beginning of David Fincher's film *Zodiac*, a young man and woman sit in the front seat of a parked car on some dimly lit waste ground. There are clearly feelings between them as the woman attempts to flirt with the man, but he senses there might be something up and he's a little nervous. Two cars full of misbehaving youths drive away, setting off fireworks as they go, startling the man and leaving the two nervous lovers alone on the wasteland. A couple of minutes after the cars have gone, another car pulls up behind them and the driver shuts off its headlights. The woman suddenly becomes very nervous, but there's something she's not telling the man. After a second, the car's headlights come back on and it speeds off.

The man asks the woman if that was her husband. She tells him it wasn't and not to worry about it. Then they hear the shrieking of tires as the car turns in the distance and drives back towards them. It parks up right behind them, blocking their car in. Someone gets out of the car with a torch, blinding the couple. The person slowly walks around to the man's window and shoots him and the woman five times before going back to the car, reloading, and coming back to shoot them again four more times. During the shooting, we never see the shooter's face, and during the dialogue, we never find out who the shooter is, although the woman clearly knows him. As the shooter returns to their own car, the scene fades to black.

This scene asks more questions that it gives answers. In fact, I don't think it answers a single question. Every line of dialogue leads to another question. Most importantly, the scene asks the question of who the shooter is. It creates a great big curiosity gap in the story. Every question asked creates a curiosity gap. This is a kind of two-for-one when it comes to your storytelling. You can set up a mystery at the start of your story, as *Zodiac* does, and you can ask questions, as *Zodiac* also does, several times over.

Your questions don't have to be at the beginning of your story either, although it's a really good starting technique because it gets your audience thinking and engaged right from the get-go. You can pepper your story with questions throughout to keep your audience engaged and to constantly create curiosity gaps throughout.

Depending on how long your story is will depend on how many you use but try to use them regularly throughout. Remember that people communicate and learn differently, so when you're asking your questions, phrase them to include everybody. For those with a kinaesthetic imagination, you could phase your question as, "Can you imagine how that would make you feel?" For those who prefer visualisation, "Imagine what that would look like," would work better. And for those with an auditory imagination, try, "Imagine you can hear the sound of..." Keep your questions open as we discussed earlier in Chapter Four.

In the scene in *Zodiac*, as the audience we know something is wrong. The person with the torch approaches the car and the young man tells the woman to get her wallet out, so he's clearly expecting them to be robbed. The surprise is that, without speaking, the person in the other car just starts shooting them. The line of dialogue sets us up to expect a robbery, so we're surprised when it turns into murder. As you can see, surprise only works if you've set up the context. We need to know what the normal world looks like, what a normal routine is for your characters. otherwise what's surprising about it? It's about establishing a pattern and then breaking it. This way, your audience thinks they know what's coming, then they find out that things aren't quite what they seem. This works with all great twists in movies.

But twists don't have to be at the end of a movie, though some of the most memorable ones are, like the dead body that's in the middle of the room throughout the entirety of *Saw* that turns out not to be dead but is in fact Jigsaw himself. So simple and brilliantly routine because you forget the body is even there after a while. Or the mundane and anti-climactic descent in the elevator in *The Departed* where Billy finally remands Colin in handcuffs only to be shot in the head the instant the elevator doors open. Blink and you'll miss it. But because of how director Martin Scorsese brings the energy out of the scene in the elevator and makes it so humdrum and normal, there's no way you're expecting what's about to happen to Billy. This is during the final third of the movie but isn't the end. Or how about something very normal indeed like eating at a diner, as in the beginning of *Pulp Fiction*, before drawing your guns on your fellow diners and holding them all to ransom?

Misdirection is also a brilliant way to widen the curiosity gap. Think about the simplest magic trick that has ever befuddled you. It's likely that through misdirection, the magician caused you to look in one direction while they did something in another direction. In magic, there are three types of misdirection. Firstly, time. The magician has done the trick ahead of time; you just don't know it. For example, they have already placed the silk handkerchief in their hand before they start the trick. Secondly, place. The magician draws your attention to their left hand while they do the trick with their right hand. And thirdly, intent. The magician will give you the illusion of free will despite leading you to a predetermined decision.

As storytellers, we can do exactly the same. We can give our audience information in a subtle way without making it overt, we can change the direction of a story mid-sentence, and we can plant clues that will lie hidden until we're ready for them to bloom.

As a storyteller, you can either misdirect your audience or you can misdirect your character and let your audience in on the misdirect.

In *The Prestige*, a film about two magicians trying to outwit each other to find the ultimate magic trick, there are so many twists and turns and misdirects that it's hard for the audience to keep up. It keeps the audience guessing throughout the film all the way until the final twist at the end. It's the same in the likes of the *Ocean's* franchise and *Inside Man*.

Films where we, the audience, know what's going on but the character has been misdirected by another character include *Snow White*, who still takes and eats the poisoned apple that causes her to fall into a coma, no matter how much we yell at the screen to ignore the evil queen disguised as the old lady with the nice shiny red apples. At the other end of the spectrum is the famous scene in *The Godfather* where Michael meets Sollozzo at Louis' Restaurant to kill him. We know because we've heard the plan to hide the gun in the bathroom that he's there to kill him, but Sollozzo doesn't. This adds to the tension and curiosity because we want to know if Michael can pull it off.

This scene also works really well because of the suspense that builds throughout it. There's the initial discussion that becomes a little heated, then Michael asks to be excused to go to the bathroom. Sollozzo stops him and pats him down to see if he has a gun. He's clearly suspicious. McClusky, the corrupt police captain who is eating with them, tells Sollozzo that he's already checked for a gun. Michael goes to the bathroom to retrieve the gun. He looks behind the cistern but initially can't find it. The sound of a passing train grows, adding to the tension. The camera cuts back to Sollozzo and McClusky looking to the bathroom, obviously suspicious that Michael is taking too long. Michael finally finds the gun and carefully takes it down from the cistern. He calmly fixes his hair and exits the bathroom.

When planning the assassination, Clemenza told Michael to come out of the bathroom shooting, but he doesn't do this (another example of surprise). Instead, he returns to the table and calmly takes his seat. Sollozzo continues talking as another train noisily passes by. As the sound of the train reaches a crescendo, Michael takes his chance and shoots both Sollozzo and McClusky before dropping the gun and leaving the restaurant. It's a masterpiece in building suspense.

All this was done by making a big promise to the audience in a previous scene – Michael's going to kill Sollozzo by coming out of the bathroom all guns blazing – but by controlling the information that the director gives the audience in terms of what is revealed and when and how he reveals it, he's able to create suspense from the beginning of the scene and ratchet it up throughout. It's about withholding the right amount of information until the opportune moment, as this scene demonstrates.

Cliff-hangers add to suspense too because of something called the 'Zeigarnik effect', or open loops. The effect occurs when an activity that has been interrupted is more easily recalled. Bluma Zeigarnik who postulated the theory suggests that people remember unfinished or interrupted tasks better than they do completed ones. As storytellers, we can play on this. Because of this natural desire for closure, we can deprive our audience of it and therefore keep them interested in our story.   Usually in a film, TV show or novel, the storyteller takes the audience to a point of action and interrupts it by switching to a more thoughtful or slower part of the story. In *The Godfather* example we have just discussed, what follows the scenario of Michael leaving the restaurant having assassinated Sollozzo is the scene of Vito leaving the hospital, returning home, and receiving visitors from the family. No action, no retribution; just room for the Zeigarnik effect to influence the audience, leaving them wanting to know what happens next. What retribution will come Michael's way? How is Michael feeling? How are the police responding to the murders? As *The Godfather* does, it's important to reward the audience's curiosity by fulfilling your promises and paying off anything that you have setup later on in the story.

In your storytelling, you might want to create an open loop by building to a crescendo. As you're about to reveal the pertinent detail, say something like, "but more on that later", before bringing the energy back down to another part of the story. You could also use phrases like, "Antwerp, Belgium, is no longer the diamond capital of the world", as the famous marketing extraordinaire Roy H Williams did for a diamond advert he created for Justice Jewellers. Immediately this sets up an open loop by making the audience think that if Antwerp isn't the diamond capital of the world anymore, then where is? It keeps them interested.

Things that are out of place also pique people's curiosity because they're incongruous. This can be something unusual happening or something that doesn't seem quite right, making the audience think, "I've got to discover how this ends". Take for instance the movie *Flight*. It's the story of a pilot who saves almost all the passengers on his plane when it malfunctions and crashes, but an investigation into the accident reveals that he was flying the plane under the influence of alcohol and cocaine. How did a man who was inebriated manage to land a plane safely after it lost power and started to nosedive towards the ground minutes after take-off, when all the other pilots that were tested in the same simulated situation, despite being completely sober, killed everyone on board? Completely incongruous, right? But it certainly opens up that curiosity gap.

Or how about in the original *Halloween* film from 1978 when Annie gets in the car in her garage. She's busy singing and doesn't notice that the windows are steamed up, but we do. It's only after a couple of seconds that she cottons on to what we've noticed, but by then it's too late. Michael Myers jumps up from the back seat and strangles her before slitting her throat. This is a genius piece of filmmaking because it makes the audience curious as to why the windows might be steamed up. It also gives the audience a little nudge so that they are a step ahead of Annie in order to build tension, because they've worked out what's coming.

As well as being incongruous, you can set up a paradox. Setting up a paradox is also a great way to keep people interested in your story. At the start of *Serpico*, we see Frank Serpico dying in the back of an ambulance with a gunshot wound to the head. In the next scene, some police officers in the police station discuss the fact that Serpico has been shot, and the fact that they "know six cops [who] said they'd like to" shoot him. Here are two pieces of conflicting information. Serpico was shot by a police officer, thus making the department corrupt, or he wasn't, but why do these police think someone would like to? Either way, we want to know more.

Since my school days, 'Of Mice and Men' has been one of my favourite novels. If, like me, you were lucky to have studied it in school, then you will no doubt be familiar with the term 'foreshadowing'. Foreshadowing is a literary device where the storyteller gives a hint of what is going to happen later on in the story, and 'Of Mice and Men' is full of it. One of the greatest TV shows ever made is also full of foreshadowing; *Breaking Bad.* And when I say full of it, I mean full of it. There's the incident where Ted Beneke trips over a rug at the start of an episode, only to then trip over it again and severely injuring his neck at the end of the show. There's also the episode when Jesse says to Jane, "you weren't supposed to wake up", when he was trying to make her breakfast in bed, and Walt and Marie laying baby Holly on her side in case she, "decides to do a little spit-up", all before Jane overdoses and chokes to death on her own vomit.

Of course, then there's Gus Fring's grisly demise and all the references to it that started a full two seasons before it happened – the reference to *The Terminator*, the pink teddy bear with half its face burnt off, and the disfigured mask among Gale's possessions, to name but a few. It's incredibly well thought through. These little moments sometimes pass us by but occasionally, and often when they're repeated, like the facial disfigurement, they start to plant themselves in our minds so we get the feeling that they mean something and that we should pay attention. It's like a trail of breadcrumbs leading the audience to where the writer wants them to go, even though they don't know where that is yet.

Success Tasks

- Write down some good open or probing questions that would work well to create a curiosity gap in your story.
- Write down three ways that you can set your story up as a mystery.
- What surprising things happen in your story? How can you make what happens before and after them seem routine, so that when the surprise happens it seems more shocking?
- Watch some magic tricks on YouTube or TV. See how the magician uses misdirection. If you're stuck for ideas, *Magic for Humans* on Netflix doesn't take itself too seriously. How can you add misdirection into your storytelling?
- What is the big promise that you make in your story? Plan out how you will release the rest of the information in your story and decide how you can withhold as much information as possible until the very last moment to build suspense.
- What open loops can you create in your story? Plan out where and when they best fit for maximum impact.
- What incongruities and paradoxes exist in your story? How can you amplify these for maximum impact?
- Plan where you can sprinkle the breadcrumbs of foreshadowing throughout your story.

The Next Level

Chapter 20: Rhetoric and Good Writing

"Good writing is supposed to evoke sensation in the
reader – not the fact that it is raining, but
the feeling of being rained upon."

– EL Doctorow, novelist

Think about the greatest stories ever told, whether they are stories delivered from a podium or those written down as prose. Which ones give you goosebumps? For me, it's a story that Tyler Perry delivered at a Volunteering and Service Conference called 'Points of Light'. He delivers his story so naturally and articulately with such poise and emotion. If you've not watched it, seek it out. I also love Barack Obama's speech that we've discussed a couple of times so far in which he tells the story about the origin of his famous 'Fired up, ready to go' chant. And consider the other great speeches from history, from Lincoln's Gettysburg Address to Martin Luther King Jr's, 'I Have a Dream' speech. Or how about some of the great literature throughout the ages? Anything that you were taught in school, from William Shakespeare and F Scott Fitzgerald to Harper Lee and, my personal favourite, John Steinbeck. What they all have in common, as well as well-told, well-structured stories, is great rhetoric – language designed to have a persuasive or impressive effect.

It's important to note from the outset of this chapter that great stories are great not because of the words used to tell them but because of the content of the story itself. That being said, I think it's safe to assume now that we're on Chapter Twenty on a book about storytelling that this is the case. Therefore, I see no harm in adding some flare to your story by ensuring that the language and rhetoric of your story, be it verbally delivered or in written form, are of the highest standard and are appropriate for the audience to whom you are speaking.

Aristotle is the father of rhetoric, first writing his treatise on the art of persuasion in the fourth century BC. In his writings, he describes three types of rhetorical appeals – ethos, logos and pathos.

Ethos is where the storyteller attempts to support their argument by backing it up with personal experience. This is all well and good when you are the smartest person in the room or you have credibility, but not so much if others in your audience are smarter or think they're smarter, or if your credibility is called into question.

Pathos is something we have covered a fair amount in this book already, where the storyteller appeals to the audience's emotions using evocative words. As we've discussed, this can be very powerful when done well but done poorly, especially using over-the-top language and too many adjectives, it can lead the audience to feel manipulated.

Logos is when the storyteller uses logic to support their argument, but as we know in our post-truth world full of 'alternative facts', logic might not always bring the result we're looking for, depending on our audience. As much as it can be about facts, it's often more about intrinsic rationale and flow of argument. If x is true, then y must follow. For example, what is the broadest statement you can get someone to agree to, and then how do you show a following stage is consistent? Rhetoric is about debate and persuasion, therefore leading someone along the path to a conclusion.

If you haven't got ethos, your audience won't trust your logos. If you haven't got pathos, they won't care about your logos. If you haven't got logos, then you have nothing to say. It isn't pick and choose; it is a triangle of collaboration.

As well as Aristotle's three rhetorical appeals, there are a great number of rhetorical devices. In fact, to my mind, there are twenty-five different forms of rhetoric device that will have an instant persuasive effect on your audience when used well (there are others, but these twenty-five will stand you in good stead without needing an MA in English). They all have fancy names but don't worry about that. The important thing is that you know what they are and how they're used. Some people, like my brother Daniel, spend years and years studying them. I have just a few pages to impart this knowledge to you, then it's up to you to put them into practice. The majority of the twenty-five you will have heard used many times before, and will most likely use already, you just won't have the fancy name. It's just a case of honing your skills so that your storytelling can be elevated to the next level.

So here goes; an alphabetical list of twenty-five types of rhetoric device and how they're used:

1. **Adynaton** is taking your exaggeration to the extreme to make a point so that what you are describing is actually impossible. Examples include, 'I'm so hungry I could eat a horse', 'when pigs fly'

and 'it's raining cats and dogs.'

2. **Alliteration** is when the same consonant sound repeats at the beginning of connected words in a sentence or phase for effect, as in *Batman Begins*, *Horton Hears a Who* and *What Women Want*.

3. **Anadiplosis** is the repetition of the last word of a sentence as the first word of the next sentence to add to the stylistic power and rhythm of the prose. Anyone familiar with *Star Wars* will know one of Master Yoda's most famous lines: "Fear leads to anger. Anger leads to hate. Hate leads to suffering."

4. **Anaphora** is when you start each sentence with the same word or phrase to emphasise a point that you want to make. There are so many examples of this in the history of great speeches, from Martin Luther King Jr's 'I Have a Dream' speech where he repeats "I have a dream" to Abraham Lincoln's second inaugural address; "With malice toward none; with charity for all; with firmness in the right..." But there's probably none more famous for using anaphora than Winston Churchill's 'We shall fight on the beaches' speech to the House of Commons in June 1940. He repeats the phrases

"we shall" and "we shall fight" over and over to drill home his point: "We shall not flag or fail. We shall go to the end. We shall fight in France, we shall fight on the seas and oceans, we shall fight with growing confidence and growing strength in the air, we shall defend our island whatever the cost may be, we shall fight on the beaches, we shall fight on the landing grounds, we shall fight in the fields and in the streets, we shall fight in the hills, we shall never surrender."

5. **Antithesis** is used for contrasting effect when two opposite ideas or images are mentioned together to emphasise them. It manages to convey more meaning than ordinary speech, for example, Neil Armstrong's famous words as he ventured out of Apollo Lunar Module 'Eagle' onto the moon on 20th July 1969, "That's one small step for man, one giant leap for mankind," is a great example of antithesis.

6. **Aposiopesis** is when you leave a sentence unfinished for emphasis, leaving the ending up to the imagination of the audience. In *Anchorman*, Ron Burgundy doesn't quite understand how this works with the phrase, "When in Rome..." but this is a good example of aposiopesis, as is "if only..."

and "or else…"

7. **Assonance** is similar to alliteration with its repeating sounds, but whereas alliteration repeats consonants at the start of words for effect, assonance repeats vowel sounds in the middle of words. In the gothic poem 'The Raven' by Edgar Allan Poe, the opening line uses assonance to great effect – 'Once upon a midnight dreary, while I pondered, weak and weary' – repeating the 'ea' sound. So does the Nat King Cole song 'Those Lazy-Hazy-Crazy Days of Summer' (repetition of 'az') and the repetition of the 'i' sound in the rhyme, 'goodnight, sleep tight, don't let the bed bugs bite.'

8. **Catachresis** is deliberate word misuse in such an obviously incorrect way that it draws attention to its use. Shakespeare loved catachresis. In 'Hamlet', Hamlet's mother decides to marry his uncle very soon after her husband has died. This is seen as inappropriate (not the marrying his uncle bit, just that not enough time has passed since her husband has died), and Hamlet is furious. He says, "I will speak daggers to her." A great use of catachresis, or mixed metaphor, that paints a brilliant picture that he will not physically kill her but will give her a stern

telling off.

9. **Chiasmus** is where there is symmetry around the middle of the sentence and the first phrase is inverted so that the concept in the first phrase is repeated in reverse order in the second phrase. You'll see this an awful lot on social media posts in an inspiring font with a picture of a beautiful sunset behind in what comedian Joe Lycett calls 'the bullshit quote'. They typically feel like they have some meaning but they don't. These are quotes like, "Do I love you because you're beautiful? Or are you beautiful because I love you?" But when done well, they look like this from John F Kennedy – "Ask not what your country can do for you, but what you can do for your country."

10. **Diacope** is when you repeat a word with one or two words in between for emphasis. Maybe the most famous examples are "Bond, James Bond" or "To be or not to be". And it's often used very well in advertising. I'm sure you've heard it in, "Maybe she's born with it. Maybe it's Maybelline", or in the Reebok slogan, "I am what I am", or said about the Energizer bunny: he "keeps going and going and going".

11. Epanalepsis is when you start and end your sentence or phrase with the same word or phrase for emphasis. "The King is dead. Long live the King." is a great example of this.

12. Epistrophe is when the same word ends successive sentences or phrases to drive a point home (the reverse of anaphora). Think about Abraham Lincoln's "of the people, by the people, for the people" in his Gettysburg Address, or Aragorn's "but that is not this day" in his rousing speech to his army outside the gates of Mordor in *The Lord of the Rings*, or even Beyonce's song 'Single Ladies', where she drives home the point that, "If you liked it then you shoulda put a ring on it."

13. Epizeuxis is the repetition of a word in immediate succession for emphasis. Consider the famous repeated line in Joseph Conrad's 'Heart of Darkness' that was retained in its movie adaptation *Apocalypse Now* – "The horror! The horror!" And how about Dylan Thomas' magnificent poem 'Do not go gentle into that good night' where he states, 'Rage, rage against the dying of the light', and Monty Python's incomparable Spam sketch where "shut up!" and "spam" are repeated over and over for emphasis and comedic effect.

14. **Hyperbaton** is to reverse the normal order of words. Frequently in hyberbaton does Master Yoda in *Star Wars* speak. "Always with you it cannot be done. You do nothing that I say. You must unlearn what you have learned. Try not! Do. Or do not. There is no try."

15. **Hyperbole** is to exaggerate in order to empathise or evoke strong feelings, or to create strong impressions. In the *Toy Story* films, Jesse tells Bullseye to "run like the wind", while in *Gone with the Wind*, Scarlett O'Hara states that, "I'll never be hungry again", and in *Frozen*, Anna sings, "For the first time in forever, there'll be music, there'll be light". Of course, in each case we know that what they're saying is vastly overstated, but we get what they're expressing within the context in which they're expressing it.

16. **Isocolon** is when successive sentences are structurally the same to maintain consistency and create balanced ideas. They have equal length, sound and rhythm. Isocolon is very popular

in poetry, even simple poetry like 'Roses are red, violets are blue.' Other examples include Muhammad Ali's famous "Float like a butterfly, sting like a bee," and Harley Davidson's slogan "American by birth. Rebel by choice."

17. **Litotes** uses irony and understatement to establish a positive by focusing on the negative, and often uses a double negative. Winnie the Pooh is described as "not the sort to give up easily." Of course, we know that means he has grit and determination, but isn't it much more lyrical and, in a funny sort of way, doesn't it give a better picture of the character?

18. **A paradox** is when you make a statement that at first seems incongruous but, upon reflection, makes sense. It is used to generate curiosity to draw your audience in and to engage their logical mind so that they can understand concepts in a different way. I love the line "Gentlemen, you can't fight in here! This is the War Room", so brilliantly delivered by Peter Sellers in *Dr Strangelove or How I Learned to Stop Worrying and Love the Bomb*. And "You never know what worse luck your bad luck has saved you from", delivered by Ellis Bell in *No Country for*

Old Men. And of course, one of the most frequently quoted lines in cinema history; "I'm going to make him an offer he can't refuse", from *The Godfather*.

19. **Personification** is giving human attributes to objects, animals and ideas to create life and motion within them. 'Thriller' by Michael Jackson is a great example of this – "Terror takes the sound" and "Horror looks you right between the eyes". Scary stuff. Logically, we know that terror and horror are emotions and can't take or look, but using this kind of language to describe fear gives it agency and brings back memories of what being terrified feels like.

20. **Rhetorical questions** are asked to create dramatic effect, to get people thinking, and to make a point rather than to get an answer. Would you watch a movie if the title was *Judge Doom Framed Roger Rabbit* or *Your Car's Behind the Mail Truck, Dude?* Probably not. It's the rhetorical question that draws you in and leaves you wanting to know more.

21. **Schesis onomaton** is technically a series of nouns and adjectives only, or any series of words that are synonymous expressions, but in reality,

it's a technique used to emphasise an idea by using different words in successive sentences that have the same meaning. My favourite example of this occurs in the Dead Parrot sketch by Monty Python when Mr Praline, played by John Cleese, is attempting to return the obviously deceased parrot to the shopkeeper, played by Michael Palin. After a series of hilarious exchanges between the two, Mr Praline finally loses his patience, explaining, "It's passed on! This parrot is no more! It has ceased to be! It's expired and gone to meet its maker! This is a late parrot! It's a stiff! Bereft of life, it rests in peace! If you hadn't nailed it to the perch it would be pushing up the daisies! It's run down the curtain and joined the choir invisible! This is an EX-PARROT!"

22. **Synaesthesia** is used to describe one of the five senses in terms of another sense. The Skittles slogan "Taste the Rainbow", the Pepsi slogan "You've never seen a taste like this" and the Coca-Cola slogan "Life tastes good" are all examples of synaesthesia.

23. **Transferred epithets** is when you take a feeling, emotion or experience and place or transfer it onto

an inanimate object, bringing it to life. For example, you could describe a dizzy man, but a height can't literally be dizzy. But by describing a height as dizzy, the height is intensifieed. You might also describe someone smoking a "nervous cigarette" or keeping a "guilty secret".

24. **Tricolon** is a type of isocolon in that successive sentences are structurally the same to maintain consistency and create balanced ideas. They have equal length, sound and rhythm, but here three is the magic number. Think "blood, sweat and tears", the famous quote from *Casablanca*, "Of all the gin-joints, in all the towns, in all the world", and "Veni, vidi, vici" ("I came, I saw, I conquered").

25. **Zeugma** uses a word once in a sentence but the word has more than one meaning. It's a great way to make your storytelling more interesting and to emphasise a point. In 'The Adventures of Tom Sawyer' by Mark Twain, Tom and a new boy get into a tussle, fall to the ground and fight well. Twain describes them as having, "covered themselves with dust and glory."

I don't know about you, but there's a lot to take in there. I bet you've come across many of them before despite not knowing the Greek and Latin terms.

The best way to learn how to implement all of this is to practise but also to consume stories at a rate of knots. Watch speeches, both historical and modern, good and bad ones. Work out why you think the rhetoric is good in the great speeches and why you think it is bad in the poor ones. Research who the speech writers are and read about their principles and techniques. Ted Sorensen wrote for John F Kennedy, and Kennedy once referred to him as his 'intellectual blood bank'. Jon Favreau (not the Marvel and *Star Wars* producer/director) wrote for Barack Obama. Martin Luther King Jr and Winston Churchill had numerous speech writers. Abraham Lincoln wrote his own speeches. There's plenty of good writing and analysis out there about their speeches.

Here's some chiasmus for you. Readers don't need to write, but writers need to read. Read everything, both fiction and non-fiction. Read good books from great authors. Read the classics. There's nothing quite like how Ernest Hemmingway, Virginia Woolf and Mark Twain structure a sentence. And read poetry, from William Shakespeare and Edgar Allan Poe to Charles Bukowski and Allen Ginsberg.

The more you watch and the more you read, the more these rhetorical devices will embed themselves into your mind and the easier it will be to recall them when you are telling your stories.

Success Tasks

- Watch Tyler Perry's 'Point of Light' speech.
- Watch Barack Obama's 'Fired up, ready to go' speech if you haven't already.

- Pick your favourite five rhetorical devices from the list and write five sentences for your story in each style.
- Watch a YouTube video of Ted Sorensen talking about how to write a good speech.
- Commit to reading a classic novel or epic poem when you have finished reading this book.

Chapter 21: Analogy and Metaphor

"The greatest thing by far is to
be a master of metaphor."
– Aristotle, Greek philosopher

In 1982, a spaceship appears and settles over Johannesburg, South Africa. Inside are over one million starving aliens, and the South African government creates a camp for them called District 9. Over the years, the camp becomes a slum, and locals regularly object to the existence of the camp complaining that the aliens are dirty, ignorant delinquents who take resources away from the humans.

Following continued disorder between the aliens and local residents, the government hire a local weapons manufacturer to move the aliens to a new camp outside the city. Wikus van de Merwe is assigned to lead the relocation taskforce.

After an incident in District 9, Wikus begins mutating into an alien. He becomes a wanted fugitive and takes refuge in the camp, but as the man who led the relocation exercise, he is hated and shunned by the aliens and has nowhere to turn. And he still continues to mutate.

A family of aliens are determined to get back to the mother ship that still hovers above the city in order to escape the slum, and Wikus offers his help.

The film *District 9* is an allegory of South African apartheid and a stark representation of the numerous refugee slums in the world today. The oppression, barbarism, subjugation and racism that takes place throughout the film is a representation of what real people go through on a daily basis in order to survive, and the film's director Neill Blomkamp dedicated his movie to refugees around the world in order to draw attention to how cruel people can be to those in need.

I deliberately excluded metaphors, analogies, allegories, parables and fables from the list of rhetorical devices in the previous chapter because they are in themselves stories to one degree or another. In short, a metaphor is a way of describing something that isn't literally true by making a comparison with something else. An analogy is a comparison between two things that have similar features in order to explain a principle or an idea. An allegory is a story that can be used to deliver a broader message from what is seemingly an unrelated narrative. A parable is a story about people that illustrates a lesson or principle and is often (but not always) moral or spiritual. A fable uses animals, plants, objects and forces of nature to illustrate a principle or lesson in a similar way to a parable.

Did all those definitions just roll into one after a couple of seconds? They did for me too, but I can assure you they are different. As you can see, they are all fairly similar in what they aim to achieve. They are all broadly a story that is symbolic of the principle that is being explained in order to explain it. So, for the sake of simplicity in this chapter, I am going to lump them all together and refer to all of them as metaphors in the tradition of NLP and use George Lakoff and Mark Johnson's definition of a metaphor – "a tool that enables people to use what they know about their direct physical and social experiences to understand more abstract things."

With this in mind, it is safe to say that the stories we tell to influence people don't always have to be true. I will caveat this by saying that if we are telling a true story about something that actually happened, then it should absolutely be true in order to maintain your integrity and keep your audience's trust. But if you are trying to instil in your audience an idea, then it is quite acceptable to resort to metaphor in order to do so. Think back to the great leaders of the past and to the stories that they told. The stories that Jesus told, those of the Oriental masters, and those of the Stoic philosophers. Metaphor has been used to inspire and influence audiences for millennia.

There are three levels of metaphor: shallow metaphors, deep metaphors and embedded metaphors.

Shallow metaphors make a simple comparison in order to create a better level of understanding within the audience. They often use an explicit comparison, such as, "This game is like watching grass grow." This takes the meaning of an understood activity (watching grass grow) with one you don't have experience of (this particular game). Often, they take the form of a simile (something is like something else) and are usually a sentence or two. Another example might be Forrest Gump's famous line, "life is like a box of chocolates," suggesting that, "you never know what you're gonna get."

Deep metaphors, on the other hand, tend to be connected to the subconscious on a greater level because they are linked more closely with human truths and how we engage with and understand the world. With deep metaphors, we can't simply practise the same principles of logic found in a literal world. They are about links, relationships and feelings. They often have more than one meaning (even if the metaphor takes the form of just one phrase or sentence) so that the story really connects with the subconscious mind. For instance, the giant chocolate fountain overflowing delicious molten Cadburys surrounded by all manner of sweet treats imploring you to dip them in that is just out of reach can suggest that our aspirations are worth pursuing rather than suggesting the need to invest in party planning equipment.

In marketing, there are considered to be seven deep metaphors. These deep metaphors can be described in just one word each, and when used properly by a brand throughout their storytelling, they can help to infiltrate customers' minds to bring a brand to life. They are balance, transformation, journey, container (inclusion/exclusion), connection, resource and control. These are universal metaphors that span countries, cultures, languages, and dialects, and help a brand to connect with their target market. As you can see, they aren't surface level metaphors; they connect on a deeper level relating to how people are connected, how they feel, how they perceive things, how they make sense of things, and ultimately, how they choose to act as a result.

To discover your brand's deep metaphor, ask a bunch of your customers to tell a story about you or your organisation and ask them to include pictures in their presentation. The pictures will allow them to be more visually descriptive. Listen carefully and don't interrupt. Find the words and phrases that they use and look for repeated and common words, phrases and images between your customers. These repetitions will point to your deep metaphor or metaphors. Which metaphor is it? Balance, transformation, journey, container (inclusion/exclusion), connection, resource or control? Is it what you expected? Does it fit into your marketplace? Does it help you stand out from your competition, or is it the same as all of them? Do you need to use it more in your storytelling to increase the gap between you and your competition, or change it to create a new conversation in your marketplace? How can you now use it more in your marketing, branding and storytelling to your advantage?

An embedded metaphor, or nested loops, is a metaphor inside a metaphor inside a metaphor. It's the *Inception* of metaphors, if you will. You start telling a story but before you complete it, you start telling another one, and before you complete that one, you start another. You then finish telling the metaphors in reverse order. The metaphors are seemingly disconnected in their content but linked in theme, so the conscious mind will shut down while trying to figure out what is going on, leaving the unconscious mind open to suggestion. It also employs the Zeigarnik effect or open loops that we discussed in Chapter Nineteen in order that the audience's natural desire for closure keeps their subconscious interested throughout the story.

For example, you might start telling the story of the three little pigs, but before the wolf gets to the house made of bricks, you interrupt your story and start telling the story of Michael Jordan's work ethic as a child. You then stop telling that story as you get to the point where Jordan was named a McDonalds All-American in high school, then tell the whole story of Vincent Van Gogh and the nine hundred paintings that he created during his lifetime. You then finish telling the story of how Michael Jordan was drafted third by the Chicago Bulls and went on to have the career he had, then finish telling how the house made of bricks wasn't blown down by the wolf. Make sense? All the stories talk about work ethic but none are related in content, so the conscious mind will shut down while trying to figure out what is going on. By leaving them unfinished, the audience's natural desire for closure keeps their subconscious interested throughout the story.

When it comes to creating the metaphor to influence the situation, it's best, as we've said all along, to begin with the end in mind. Identify the outcome you want to achieve. It's also a good idea to understand how the people involved in this outcome will react, behave and feel when this result is achieved. The next thing to note in more detail is the issue at hand. What's the current problem, who's involved, what roles do they play in the problem, and how is everyone currently feeling?

Next, it's time to identify what's called a 'content layer' that will properly reflect the structure of the problem. Not only does the content layer need to reflect the structure but it also has to interest your audience, so you need to know who your audience is. Will your content layer be sporting, ancient mythology, a fairy tale, a scene from a movie, a historical figure, or your family?

If your audience loves sport, then the Michael Jordan example from above would be an excellent sporting content layer to wrap your metaphor in. If your audience are all children, then a fairy tale content layer might work well. After all, we've been telling fairy tales for centuries, possibly as far back as the Bronze Age, to help children understand what it means to be human and to help them get to grips with the world around them, including to teach them about danger. However, if your audience are all likely to be parents, then sharing a story about your family to act as your content layer to mirror what you are trying to explain will work well.

Once you've decided what your content layer is, you will

need to find or create an example that mirrors the problem you have and the outcome you desire in the content layers. This means that the story that takes place is structurally similar to the problem, relationships and context that you are trying to help them overcome, as well as the processes of achieving the outcome.

When you've completed composing your metaphor, it's a good idea to test it on someone you trust so as to avoid misunderstanding. If they're not carefully constructed and delivered, it's easy for metaphors to be misconstrued and a different interpretation to be reached, and therefore a different outcome to be inadvertently realised. And you don't want that. If your test audience misunderstands or you can see that they're slightly confused in places, refine the metaphor until it's clear and precise with no danger of being misinterpreted.

Success Tasks

- Watch *District 9* or pick a fable by Aesop, a fairy tale by the Brothers Grimm, a Sufi tale, or one of Jesus' parables to read. Note how it is structured, as suggested above, to make the point that the storyteller is attempting to get across.
- Ask your customers to help you to identify your brand's deep metaphor – is it balance, transformation, journey, container (inclusion/exclusion), connection, resource or control? Why did you pick that one?

- If you were going to tell your story as a metaphor rather than a true story, what content layer would you use and why?
- Write your story as a metaphor.

Chapter 22: Live and Relive

"You've got to relive your story: like you're right there, experiencing it right now."

– Dr Ivan Misner, Founder of BNI and author

What's it like when you experience someone telling you something and you can tell that their heart's not in it? You don't buy into it, right? Why is that? It's because you feel that they don't buy into it either.

In the film *Inception* when Cobb is instructing Ariadne on how to construct a dream whilst inside a dream of his own, Ariadne asks Cobb who the people in the dream world are. Cobb explains that they are projections of his subconscious. As Ariadne stops just being a part of the dream world and starts to experiment, playing with the physics and causing Paris to fold in on itself, creating new walkways and bridges from her own experience, she starts to stand out to the people in Cobb's dream and they begin to watch her with suspicion.

Ariadne asks Cobb why they're looking at her. Cobb explains that his subconscious feels that something is not quite right and has begun to realise that someone else is creating the world of the dream, and that the less she is simply a part of the dream and the more she changes things, the more the projections of his subconscious become suspicious. This suspicion grows and grows until eventually they attack her and she has to be pulled out of the dream.

It's the same with your storytelling. If you are not entirely a part of your story, then your audience quickly becomes aware that something is not quite right. They stop engaging and trusting in the veracity of the story you are telling.

So, when you tell your story, whether it's the first time or the one hundred and first time of telling it, whether it's delivered orally or in written form, you have to become a part of the story. You have to live the story as if it's happening to you there and then. If it's a story that you have experienced, you have to relive it. If it's a story that you're recounting that someone else has experienced, you have to draw on all your empathy and live it as if you were that person. And if it's a metaphor that you have created, then you have to put yourself in the protagonist's shoes and live it as if you were there, even if the main character is a plant, an animal or a mythical creature. By doing this, you can truly connect with how the character felt during the story, how the characters looked and behaved, how the circumstances interacted with your senses, and how the conflict and the changes made you and the other characters feel.

This is essentially an internal preparation exercise where you take some time to consider everything that we have discussed in this book so far. Go through each stage of your story imagining how everything looked, felt and sounded. In particular, take a few moments to become each of your characters, to really feel how they felt during each moment of the story.

There is an element of vulnerability to this preparation, and if you are delivering your story orally, there is vulnerability in its delivery too. By being vulnerable, I don't mean it's necessary to share all of your deepest, darkest secrets, or to break down crying when you tell your story. What I mean is that you need to find a conscious and genuine openness, an authenticity and commitment to share your story with passion and enthusiasm, and to include all the elements that we have discussed throughout this book. To truly connect with your audience, you must live and relive your story every time you tell it, otherwise you will be caught out and will not get the results you want it to produce.

Success Tasks

- Watch the clip from *Inception* where Ariadne learns how to build dreams.
- Take some time to prepare the delivery of your story, imagining each stage in terms of how it would feel, how it would look, and how it would sound. Become your characters and feel what they felt at each stage of the story.
- If your story is one you deliver regularly, monitor your delivery of it so that it doesn't become stale. If you find it becoming stale, refresh it by carrying out task two again and the next time you deliver it, inject some more energy.

Chapter 23: How to Collect Stories

"To observe attentively is to remember distinctly."

– Edgar Allan Poe, writer, poet, editor and literary critic

Growing up, my favourite filmmaker was Tim Burton and I still adore his early work, from *Edward Scissorhands* and *Beetlejuice* to *Batman* and *Sleepy Hollow*. I love the way that Burton tells his stories – the feel of them, the larger-than-life characters, the way the films look, the music. And how, when all these things are done well as Tim Burton does them, the film becomes greater than the sum of its parts.

I also love his film *Big Fish*. It tells the story of Will Bloom who returns home to care for his dying father, Edward. Edward is a raconteur and throughout Will's life, he has had a proclivity for telling amazing and somewhat fantastical stories, none of which Will has ever believed. Now, at the end of Edward's life, Will decides to investigate if any of the stories his father has told were ever really true.

The skill that Edward has throughout the film and that all good storytellers have is that they collect stories wherever they go. They do this by being curious – being in the moment, watching, asking questions, listening, paying attention, being empathetic, and being open-minded.

When a giant comes to the town where Edward lives and starts to eat all the cattle, Edward doesn't hide like the rest of the townsfolk for fear of being eaten himself. Instead, he becomes curious and remains open-minded, seeking out the giant. By talking with him and seeing the situation from the giant's point of view, he discovers that the giant doesn't want to eat people, just sheep, because he's hungry and it takes a lot of food to feed him on account of him being so big.

Edward talks the giant, called Carl, into leaving to protect the town's livestock and economy, and Edward decides to leave with him. Together they set off on a series of adventures. Without his initial curiosity and open-mindedness, Edward would never have a story about meeting a giant to share with people, would never have collected Carl's stories from his life, and would never have set off on adventures around the world, which lead to a whole collection of other stories for him to tell.

As well as staying curious in order that you experience as much of life as possible to collect your own stories and the stories of others, it is important to read and watch everything, and not just everything within your comfort zone. Different cultures tell stories differently, so it's important to take in stories from various parts of the world as well as where you were brought up. It's amazing how storytelling changes from place to place.

Some of my favourite films are not in the English language – in fact, six of my all-time top ten are not. My favourite film of all time is *The Great Beauty*, an Italian film set in Rome about an aging playboy who changes the way he sees life after his sixty-fifth birthday. I also love *Ida*, a Polish film about a nun who is about to take her vows but uncovers a family secret dating back to the Nazi occupation of Poland. *Leviathan* is another favourite of mine, a crime drama about family and corruption set in a small costal town on the northern coast of Russia. *Once Upon a Time in Anatolia*, a Turkish crime drama about a group of men who set out into the Anatolian steppes in search of a dead body, is another of my favourites. *Tabu* is a Portuguese romantic silent film from 2012 that I love about a lady who teams up with her dead neighbour's maid to find a man who has a secret connection to her past life as a farm owner in Africa. And *Timbuktu*, a Malian drama about a cattle herder and his family whose quiet lives are disturbed when jihadists try to take over their town, completes the selection.

As well as seeking out stories from different cultures to yours, it's important to take in stories in different formats than you are used to. If you would usually read a novel, try reading a graphic novel. If you would usually watch a narrative movie, try watching a documentary. And if you would normally watch a live-action film, try an animated film. If you can, do a bit of it all. An animated film in a different language – for me this would be something by the amazing Studio Ghibli in Japan, creators of *Spirited Away*, *Princess Mononoke* and *The Wind Rises*, to name but a few. Every film they have ever produced has mesmerised me. Or watch a documentary in a different language. *The Act of Killing*, an Indonesian documentary about the people who took part in the Indonesian mass killings of 1965-1966, is mind-blowing.

We're also used to hearing the fairy tales and mythologies that we were told as children. For me, these are very Eurocentric; the Germanic and Norse fairy tales of the Brothers Grimm and Hans Christian Anderson. Through school, I was taught the mythology of ancient Greece and ancient Rome. But by educating myself in African and Eastern mythology, I have come to appreciate an entirely different approach to storytelling, and a whole host of characters and folklore that I was unaware of.

The other thing that's important to read is the news. Not the daily news that's on an infinite fifteen-minute loop of the same two or three stories but the news from around the world from different news sources. Read The Guardian, The New York Times, Spiegel and Le Monde, and listen to NPR and BBC World News. But also find other news sources that you wouldn't usually pay attention to. News that perhaps you wouldn't seek out in order to inform yourself but news that you can find stories in to inform your storytelling.

Local news is always full of interesting stories that never make the national or international news, and there's no local news like Florida local news, to the point where there is now an internet meme called 'Florida Man'. Essentially, because of Florida's supposed infamy for bizarre and unusual events, news articles about peculiar crimes or events occurring in Florida, especially those with 'Florida Man' in the headline, started making their way online in 2013 as part of a game. The game is about finding the strangest headline to include the words 'Florida Man'. Simply type it into Google and see what comes up. It's sometimes quite amusing, sometimes quite frightening, and at other times really rather sad. Here are a few of my favourites that are safe for publication.

'Florida Man charged with assault with a deadly weapon after throwing alligator through Wendy's drive-thru window.'

'Florida Man admits killing goat and drinking its blood for pagan sacrifice, would still like to be senator.'

'Florida Man disguises himself in bull costume as he tries to burn down former lover's house with pasta sauce.'

'Florida man gets tired of waiting at hospital, steals ambulance, drives home.'

'Florida Man denies drinking and driving, says he only swigged bourbon at stop signs.'

How great are these? And if not turning points for stories, they could certainly make for great details or scenes in stories.

I once took a screenwriting class where we were encouraged to buy five newspapers from that week and find ten stories that grabbed our attention that might make for a compelling script. The same can be done with any of the 'Florida Man' headlines, and you can do something similar with any number of the stories that make the news around the world on a daily basis.

Once you have experienced your own stories, those of others or read or watched stories from around the world, it's time to organise your stories into a story bank. To begin with, you may want to keep a small notebook and pen on you, or download a note app to your phone and create a section in the app to collect your stories in. I use Google Keep with a hashtag #storybank because it's free and easily syncs to my desktop, but there are plenty of other notetaking apps available. Every time you hear or experience a good story, make a note of it. Keep your notebook or app by your bed – it's amazing how often a story will come back to you at two o'clock in the morning, or how often a dream can form part of a good story.

As part of your regular routine, you need to move the notes from your notebook or note app into your story bank. Your story bank is a catalogue of all your stories. It doesn't have to be anything complicated, it just needs to be a central location where you keep all your stories with all your story development. I like to use a simple spreadsheet. Start by noting down the basic plot. Across the top row are the categories that we have discussed in the book, from audience and emotions all the way through the eleven Cs and rhetoric. This gives you a really simple way to develop your story in the right way and include all the principles to ensure that you connect with your correct audience on as deep a level as humanly possible. I have created a template of a story bank that you can download for free. Go to www.weareopusmedia. com/ruletheworld to begin using it today.

Once you have developed your collected stories using all the elements in this book, you should take it one step further by writing each of your stories out as prose in a document. This helps you to flesh out each of your stories to the length that it needs to be. This is a useful exercise to ensure that you are making the best use of each element in order to grab your audience's attention and improve your descriptions of characters and circumstances, your conversational elements, and your rhetorical devices.

Think about any film you've ever seen. If the script hadn't been written down, what would the outcome of the movie have been? It probably wouldn't have been any good. The cast wouldn't have known what to say and do, the production designer wouldn't have known what sets to build, the property master wouldn't have known what props the actors needed to interact with, the costume designer wouldn't have known what the cast should be wearing, the director wouldn't have known how to pull it all together, and the producer would have had nothing to sell in order to raise finance.

Think back to the best stand-up comics you've ever seen on a TV or Netflix special. Have you ever noticed that the audience on the front row changes regularly throughout the special? I noticed this recently when I was watching Dave Chapelle's latest. And I noticed that the audience on the front row changed mid-joke too. This just goes to show how well rehearsed Chapelle's routine is, that he can deliver the same stories and the same jokes over two shows and can cut and switch the recording mid- joke without his flow being interrupted. The only way to do this is to work from a script and practise until it is flawless.

Success Tasks

- Practise your curiosity with a member of your family or a friend that you don't know as well as you would like. Ask them about their life before you knew them.
- Remember to stay in the moment, ask questions, listen, pay attention, be empathetic and remain open-minded.
- Watch a film not in your native language to see how the storytelling is different, ideally something that was made by filmmakers from a different continent from you.
- Buy a newspaper that you wouldn't usually buy. Circle ten stories that stand out to you that would be compelling to expand and tell in the future, even if you don't yet know in what context.
- Buy a small notebook or download a notetaking app to your phone.
- Download your free story bank spreadsheet at

www.weareopusmedia.com/ruletheworld

- Put all the elements of your story into the story bank spreadsheet.
- Write your story out as prose.

Chapter 24: What's Your Story?

"Your brand is a story unfolding across
all customer touch points."

– Jonah Sachs, storyteller, author, designer and entrepreneur

Now that you have all the component parts of how to tell a good story in place, it's time to build a culture of storytelling in your organisation. After all, as Peter Drucker once said, "culture eats strategy for breakfast." It's all well and good having one great story that you can reel off verbatim that includes everything that we've talked about in this book, but if that's as far as you take it, then the principles you've learned fall down there. You need to ensure that storytelling permeates your organisation at every level and that these principles are used every time a story is told.

The stories you and your team tell internally are the biggest human indicators of the health of your organisation. Eventually, the stories you tell internally will become the same stories that are told externally.

In the wild, two species of animals treat their sick and injured very differently. Penguins attack and kill their injured because they can't afford for their flock to be held back in their bid for survival in the cold winter. Elephants, on the other hand, help, support and nurture their injured back to full health. Imagine telling this story to your team. Which animal you then compare your organisation to will make a huge difference to the outcome of the story, how the rest of the team feel, and the story that will ripple through your ranks and out into the world.

If you compare your organisation to penguins, you're saying to your team that you're competitive and you don't care about people, that the team aren't appreciated, and that they are expendable. How do you think the team will feel? Once this story gets out into the world, how do you think your customers and your competitors will feel? Alternatively, if you compare your organisation to the elephants, you're saying that you're supportive and you care about people, that the team are appreciated, and that they are family. How do you think the staff will feel in this case? Once this story gets out into the world, how do you think your customers and your competitors will feel? Very different, right?

You can see how easy it is for stories to shape the culture and perception of your organisation, and once this happens, some of your marketing takes care of itself, good or bad.

Because we know that stories are so powerful, we need to make sure that we are telling the right stories to set a solid cultural foundation. Create the culture you want in your organisation by telling stories that set the tone internally, and the stories will find their way out. That's how you make a real difference to the lives of the people around you.

Build your organisation around your mythology and stories.

By creating an identity for your organisation through strong and clear storytelling, and by telling a story internally that your potential customers can easily identify with and relate to, you will demonstrate authenticity in your organisation as the story permeates outwards. This allows customers to express their sense of self by buying your products or services or associating themselves with your brand.

It then comes down to creating different versions of your stories for different media and different purposes. The same goes for your story that you have been working on throughout this book.

When I pitch a movie, I have to be able to sell it by presenting it in versions of different lengths. Firstly, I need a logline. A logline is one sentence that summarises the central conflict of my story whilst also giving an idea of a story synopsis, the characters, and the emotional arc of the story in order to grab immediate interest. This is a really hard thing to do – to take months of work and a movie that you're so close to, with all of its intricacies and subtleties, and to condense it into one sentence, but it's important. Here are a few famous loglines. See if you can guess the movie and consider how well the filmmakers did at summarising their films in one sentence.

A young FBI cadet must confide in an incarcerated and manipulative killer to receive his help on catching another serial killer who skins his victims.

With the help of a German bounty hunter, a freed slave sets out to rescue his wife from a brutal Mississippi plantation owner.

During the US-Vietnam War, Captain Willard is sent on a dangerous mission into Cambodia to assassinate a renegade colonel who has set himself up as a god among a local tribe.

A Las Vegas-set comedy centred around three groomsmen who lose their about-to-be-wed buddy during their drunken misadventures then must retrace their steps in order to find him.

A former Roman general sets out to exact vengeance against the corrupt emperor who murdered his family and sent him into slavery.

If you were the studio executive having just been pitched these movies, could you say no to hearing more about any of them? I certainly couldn't. They are of course *The Silence of the Lambs*, *Django Unchained*, *Apocalypse Now*, *The Hangover* and *Gladiator*. Outside of the film world, great brands can often do this with single benefit-driven words and slogans. Take the following brands for example: Harley-Davidson defines themselves as freedom, Lego as imagination, and Estee Lauder as beauty. Apple's slogan is 'Think Different', Levi's is 'Quality never goes out of style', and Disneyland's is 'The happiest place on Earth'. Donald Trump's slogan, "Make America Great Again", (which, by the way, uses the majority of the principles in the book – I told you he was a great storyteller) fitted on a hat. What's on your hat?

The next thing I need when pitching a movie is my elevator pitch. This is the sixty-second version of the story that gets across the salient details – conflict, story arc, emotional arc and characters, as well as the feel and tone of the story. You need this version of your stories too. This is also difficult because you know all the details of your story that you've worked on throughout the book and you're now cutting it down without losing the essence of what you've created. That being said, if Donald Trump can incorporate nine of the eleven Cs in four words to stick on a hat, as well as deliver a benefit, imply emotion and make his target audience the hero, then I'm sure you can manage to include the principles that you've planned into your story in sixty seconds.

Once you've completed your sixty-second version of your story you can then flesh it out as I do in my film pitches. A three-minute version, a ten-minute version and, if you are going to be presenting on stage, perhaps a thirty-minute version. This allows you to develop the benefits you offer, the feel of the story, the emotions, the characters, the world the characters inhabit, their motivations, and what's at stake.

When I have completed writing all the versions of my story, I also have to produce a mood board to show to the executive to whom I'm pitching. A mood board is a visual representation of how we envisage the film to look and feel. It's a good idea for you to do the same for your stories. Can you distil your story to just one or a few images? If so, what are they, and why have you chosen them? How do these images inform the way you have written your stories? How do they symbolise the benefits that you offer? Do you need to go back and rewrite a section or a character? Do you need to change a description of the time or place?

Once these stories and images have then been disseminated through your team, been written up on your websites and social channels, then presented in your sales meetings and in your presentations on stage, you will start to see a brand community develop around your stories and around your mythology. This community will be loyal to you not because of what you sell but because of the connection to your story and mythology, and the community will begin to grow. When this happens, it's because your storytelling is resonating with your customers' core values.

Success Tasks

- What stories do you need to tell within your organisation to establish a culture of storytelling?
- What stories do you need to teach your team in order that you have a consistent bank of stories permeating

from within your organisation to build your brand's mythology?

- Write a logline, a sixty-second, three-minute, ten-minute and thirty-minute version of your story.
- Find an image or images that represent your story.

Final Thoughts

Final Thoughts

"Storytelling is the most powerful way to
put ideas into the world."

– Robert McKee, author, lecturer and story consultant

It's just before lunchtime on the 7th November 2020. Donald Trump, in a state of denial, is on his golf course in Virginia. The Associated Press and a slew of other media outlets have just called the election for Joe Biden, an outcome that had looked likely for the past few days. President Trump releases a statement declaring the election "far from over" and falsely accuses President-Elect Biden of undermining the electoral process. This is a very different look from the celebrations of four years ago.

Meanwhile, in his hometown of Wilmington, Delaware, the mood couldn't be more different.

President-Elect Joseph R Biden and Vice-President-Elect Kamala Harris take the stage wearing masks due to the Coronavirus pandemic to address a carpark populated with flag-waving, car-horn-tooting supporters also wearing masks. Probably not the victory speech he had dreamed of since he entered politics some forty-eight years earlier, although it did allow for a firework display at the end. Both Biden and Harris called for unity and to "give each other a chance".

How could this have happened? All the stories and promises made by President Trump just four years earlier and all the mass inspiration and influence that he had: gone, just like that.

Again, my answer is fairly straightforward and probably oversimplified, but I'll give it to you anyway.

Being able to build the future with stories requires that the right stories have been told in the past. And if you've told the right stories in the past, you need to continue to tell the right stories to build the future. This takes planning, thought and humility, and President Trump didn't have his balance right. His past stories didn't match his future stories. His past stories promised too much compared to his future stories.

Hopefully, you agree that stories are powerful tools that can be used to inspire and influence people. If you didn't before you read this book, I certainly hope that you do now. And with that in mind, I must implore you to use your storytelling skills carefully and only ever for good. In the words of Uncle Ben from *Spiderman*, "With great power comes great responsibility."

Too many people throughout history have used their ability as great storytellers to bring about evil in the world, and I'm not suggesting for a minute that you would do the same, but it is possible to use good storytelling for manipulative purposes to bring about selfish gain to the detriment of others.

On the other hand, as we have seen throughout the real-life examples in this book and many others throughout history, great storytelling has unbelievable power to bring about immeasurable good. Please use your new skills for this purpose.

And finally, remember that you are the collection of stories you tell yourself. The existing condition of your life is a direct consequence of these stories. If you tell yourself the story that you are not good enough, then that's what you will believe and that is what will manifest itself in all areas of your life – your family life, your job, your social life. If you tell yourself the story that you are good enough, the opposite will be true. It's as Henry Ford said, "Whether you think you can, or you think you can't – you're right." If you want to change your life, you need to change the stories that you tell yourself.

Success Tasks

- Plan the stories you are going to tell so that you have balance in your past stories and your future stories.
- Check in with the stories that you currently tell and plan to tell in the future. Are they for good? If not, should you be telling them?
- What stories do you tell yourself? Do you need to change any of them? If so, identify a new story to replace the story you are going to stop telling yourself and take action to begin telling it to yourself immediately.

Resources

To download the character development sheet, plot point/emotion matrix, story bank template, and to find a link to our podcast 'Rule the World; the art and power of storytelling' along with many other tools to help you tell stories to inspire, influence and succeed please visit www.weareopusmedia.com/ruletheworld

Success Tasks by Chapter

Chapter 1: Why Story?

- Search Google for the Liang Bulu'Sipong 4 cave painting.
- Look for a random pattern in your home or office. Make up a story about what's happening in the pattern.
- Below is a list of ten random words. Make up a story mnemonic to remember them all.

Juror	Snack
Trifle	Wife
Plane	Lawnmower
Juggler	Egg
Flame	Swarm

- Read the Gettysburg Address, Martin Luther King Jr's 'I Have a Dream' speech or the parable of the Prodigal Son (it can be found in the Bible in the Book of Luke, Chapter 15, Verses 11-32).
- Watch *Inception*.

Chapter 2: Who's Your Audience?

- Watch your favourite film again. What is the main character's want? What is their need? How do the filmmakers play them off against each other for dramatic effect? How does this juxtaposition of want versus need resolve at the end of the film?

- Write a list of ten visual words, ten auditory words and ten kinaesthetic words.
- Take a VARK test online to understand what type of learner/communicator you are.
- Take a DISC test online to understand your profile.
- Look at your diary. When is the story that came to mind when you read the introduction next likely to be delivered? Do some research into the person or people that you will be presenting to before you come face-to-face with them. How much can you find out about them to help you prepare your story in terms of their communication styles and their demographic, psychographic, behavioural and geographic profiles?

Chapter 3: Begin with the End in Mind

- Write down the outcomes you want from your audience after you've told them your story.

Chapter 4: How to Grab Attention

- Watch the Blake scene from *Glengarry Glen Ross* (it can be found on YouTube) or for that matter, watch the whole film.
- Write five opening lines for your story that start in on the action.

- Write five questions that could work well at the beginning of your story.
- Again, find five ways to open your story provocatively.
- Find five ways to start your story using pictorial language.
- Find five ways to start your story from an emotional place.
- Write a trailer for your story.

Chapter 5: Story Structure

- Watch *The Matrix* with this chapter open to see where these moments happen.
- Watch one other film and see if you can work out where each of the moments happen for each of the three models (two turning points, nine plot points and twelve plot points). An action/adventure film will be pretty easy, or stretch yourself and try it with something more comedy-, romance- or drama-based.
- Write the beats out for your story for each of these three models.
- Think back to the last ten films or TV shows you've watched. What story arc did they each fit into?
- How about the last novel you read? What story arc did that fit into?
- Which story arc does your story fit into? Write out your story following one of the examples within your

respective story arc.

Chapter 6: So What?

- Check your diary for your next three meetings. What are your desired outcomes for these meetings?
- List ten benefits for each of these outcomes. Make sure to include pain prevention and gain benefits.
- Work out what story is suitable for each of these benefits, be it a story you've been involved in, a story you've heard, or a metaphor or allegory.
- Take a look at the story you tell regularly. Are you using it in the right context with the right benefits for the right audience?

Chapter 7: Emotion

- Watch *Scrubs* Season Four, Episode Eight: 'My Last Chance'.
- Watch *The West Wing* Season One, Episode Ten: 'In Excelsis Deo'.
- Watch a bunch of Christmas TV adverts, including the 2020 Amazon advert entitled 'The Show Must Go On'.
- Write up your plot point/emotion matrix for your story.

Chapter 8: Who's the Hero?

- Watch *The Lord of the Rings* or at least some clips of Gandalf on YouTube (I know they are long films).

- Google search 'solicitors' and try and find one that makes their customers the hero of the story on their website.
- Watch the #HowToDad Peanut Butter Cheerios ad on YouTube.
- Go back over your story and work out who the hero is. If you're involved, is it you or the person you're helping? If it's you, shift it so that the person you're helping becomes the hero and you come across as the mentor with authority and empathy, and that you call them to action and give them a plan, and that you're there throughout the journey, just like Gandalf.

Chapter 9: Character

- Watch the entrances described in the screenplays above and see how nailed-on the actors' performances are to the descriptions.
- This is a deep one but bear with me. Write down a list of your strengths and weaknesses and how they are linked with your beliefs, motivations, ambitions and fears.
- Watch an episode or two of *The Wire* or *The Boys* to see how the lines between good and bad are blurred and how interesting conflicted characters can be.
- Watch the speeches from *The Empire Strikes Back*, Apocalypse Now and *Django Unchained*.
- Look back at your emotion matrix from chapter

Seven to refresh your memory on how each of your characters are feeling at each beat of your story.

- Create a character sheet for each of your characters based on the topics discussed in this chapter.

Chapter 10: Circumstance

- The next time you watch a film, keep an eye out for great imagery that means more than just what is in the frame. When you spot something, pause the film and snap a quick picture on your phone to remember it.
- Watch the diner scene from *Mulholland Drive* with the sound on and with the sound off. See and hear the difference that sound makes.
- Visit a 4D experience near you.
- Watch an episode of a cookery show of your choice. Pay attention to how your digestive system switches on and how you become more involved in the show because of it.
- Write five short descriptions of where your story takes place using the five senses.

Chapter 11: Context

- Next time you watch a film or TV show, write down all the contextual elements that, if they were removed, would mean that the story didn't make sense or would make the characters or situations less engaging. What do you notice about them?

- What connection points can you create in your story by including relevant context?

Chapter 12: Conflict

- Watch the trailer for *The Silence of the Lambs*.
- What's at stake for the characters in your story? Write a list of five things for each character and don't stop until you've got five.
- What motivates your character? Pain or gain?
- What obstacles can you throw at your character to demotivate them and test their mettle?
- What conflict can you set up early in your story and hang onto to increase the tension, in order to pay it off later?
- What are the external and internal conflicts in your story? What's the ideological conflict in your story?
- Who's the villain in your story? Why are they the villain? If the villain is a person, what do they believe? If the villain is not a person, what form does the villain take?

Chapter 13: Cure

- Look at some brands that you admire. See how few words they use to describe what they do.
- Write down what you do in the fewest number of

words you can.

- In your story, what was the cure that took your client or team member from conflict to change? And in how few words can you write this down?

Chapter 14: Change

- Pick a happy defining moment in your life. How have your circumstances changed as a result of that moment? What emotional shift has taken place because of that moment? How do you feel now compared to before?
- Write down ten ways that you make a difference in the lives of your clients. - What problems do you solve? What outcomes do you deliver?
- Re-read chapters Seven to Ten.
- How have the lives of the characters in your story changed as a result of the cure that was applied, both in terms of circumstance and emotion?

Chapter 15: Carry-Out Message

- Watch Obama's 'Fired up, ready to go' speech.
- Make a note of the locations of all your upcoming meetings and presentations for the next month. Also note how busy the audience is likely to be. Will you have the luxury to allow your stories to hang for your audience's subconsciouses to interpret the story on a deeper level and take action, or will you need to tell

the audience the carry-out message?

- Write three succinct carry-out messages for your story. Until it's well practiced, the sentence will probably start, "The reason I tell you this story is…"

Chapter 16: Call to Action

- Write three calls to action that include all the principles that we've discussed and A/B test them over your next fifteen presentations to see which gives you better results.

Chapter 17: Conversation

- Pinpoint the emotional high and low points in your story. Who is involved? What conversations took place between these people? What one or two lines of dialogue were the most important in this conversation?
- Check that your dialogue serves one of the three purposes that we have discussed – moves story forward, shows character, or builds relationship.
- Write down this famous line of movie dialogue from *On the Waterfront* as said by each of your characters, ensuring that it is distinct for each of their voices: "You don't understand! I could've had class. I could've been a contender. I could've been somebody, instead of a bum, which is what I am."
- How do your characters speak their lines of dialogue?

Whisper? Announce? Pontificate? Or something else? And what are their posture, eye contact, mannerisms, reactions and emotions like when they're talking and being spoken to?

- Write down any dialogue that you have chosen to include in your story and make sure that it uses a unique voice.
- Remove the first few words from each line of dialogue until it doesn't make sense anymore.
- Read your dialogue out loud and amend it so that it flows smoothly off your tongue.

Chapter 18: Comedy

- If you haven't already watched the 'Fired up, ready to go' speech by Barack Obama, go and watch it.
- Buy a 'word of the day' calendar or subscribe to a word of the day email to improve your vocabulary.
- Analyse your style of humour. What style (or styles) do you have? What styles don't you have? Watch a stand-up special from a comedian with a similar style to you and analyse how what they deliver works.
- Go and sit in a busy place and observe what is happening for an hour. Take a notebook and write down as much as you can about the people you see (conversations, interactions, what they do, etc.). Once you get home, go back through your notes

and highlight anything that stands out as funny, fundamental to the human experience, or which connects with you on a personal level. Pick one idea and write ten jokes from it using the setup, anticipation, and punchline formula. They don't have to be good. Just write them. Don't stop until you have ten.

- Carry out the 'Yes, and' exercise to the humour in your story.
- Practise the jokes in your story out loud to your closest family and friends, or to a small focus group.
- Decide which elements of your story can work as a call-back.
- Analyse your audience for your next five meetings. What elements of humour will be appropriate?

Chapter 19: Curiosity

- Write down some good open or probing questions that would work well to create a curiosity gap in your story.
- Write down three ways that you can set your story up as a mystery.
- What surprising things happen in your story? How can you make what happens before and after them seem routine, so that when the surprise happens, it seems more shocking?
- Watch some magic tricks on YouTube or TV. See how the magician uses misdirection. If you're stuck for

ideas, *Magic for Humans* on Netflix doesn't take itself too seriously. How can you add misdirection into your storytelling?

- What is the big promise that you make in your story? Plan out how you will release the rest of the information in your story and decide how you can withhold as much information as possible until the very last moment to build suspense.
- What open loops can you create in your story? Plan out where and when they best fit for maximum impact.
- What incongruities and paradoxes exist in your story? How can you amplify these for maximum impact?
- Plan where you can sprinkle the breadcrumbs of foreshadowing throughout your story.

Chapter 20: Rhetoric and Good Writing

- Watch Tyler Perry's 'Point of Light' speech.
- Watch Barack Obama's 'Fired up, ready to go' speech if you haven't already.
- Pick your favourite five rhetorical devices from the list and write five sentences for your story in each style.
- Watch a YouTube video of Ted Sorensen talking about how to write a good speech.
- Commit to reading a classic novel or epic poem when you have finished reading this book.

Chapter 21: Analogy and Metaphor

- Watch *District 9* or pick a fable by Aesop, a fairy tale by the Brothers Grimm, a Sufi tale, or one of Jesus' parables to read. Note how it is structured, as suggested above, to make the point that the storyteller is attempting to get across.
- Ask your customers to help you to identify your brand's deep metaphor – is it balance, transformation, journey, container (inclusion/exclusion), connection, resource or control? Why did you pick that one?
- If you were going to tell your story as a metaphor rather than a true story, what content layer would you use and why?
- Write your story as a metaphor.

Chapter 22: Live and Relive

- Watch the clip from *Inception* where Ariadne learns how to build dreams.
- Take some time to prepare the delivery of your story, imagining each stage in terms of how it would feel, how it would look, and how it would sound. Become your characters and feel what they felt at each stage of the story.
- If your story is one you deliver regularly, monitor your delivery of it so that it doesn't become stale. If you find it becoming stale, refresh it by carrying out Task

Two again and the next time you deliver it, inject some
more energy.

Chapter 23: How to Collect Stories

- Practise your curiosity with a member of your family or
  a friend that you don't know as well as you would like.
  Ask them about their life before you knew them.
- Remember to stay in the moment, ask questions,
  listen, pay attention, be empathetic and remain open-
  minded.
- Watch a film not in your native language to see how
  the storytelling is different, ideally something that was
  made by filmmakers from a different continent from
  you.
- Buy a newspaper that you wouldn't usually buy.
  Circle ten stories that stand out to you that would be
  compelling to expand and tell in the future, even if you
  don't yet know in what context.
- Buy a small notebook or download a notetaking app to
  your phone.
- Download your free story bank spreadsheet at
  www.weareopusmedia.com/ruletheworld
- Put all the elements of your story into the story bank
  spreadsheet.
- Write your story out as prose.

Chapter 24: What's Your Story?

- What stories do you need to tell within your organisation to establish a culture of storytelling?
- What stories do you need to teach your team in order that you have a consistent bank of stories permeating from within your organisation to build your brand's mythology?
- Write a logline, a sixty-second, three-minute, ten-minute and thirty-minute version of your story.
- Find an image or images that represent your story.

Final Thoughts

- Plan the stories you are going to tell so that you have balance in your past stories and your future stories.
- Check in with the stories that you currently tell and plan to tell in the future. Are they for good? If not, should you be telling them?
- What stories do you tell yourself? Do you need to change any of them? If so, identify a new story to replace the story you are going to stop telling yourself and take action to begin telling it to yourself immediately.

Acknowledgments

Firstly, I would like to thank my wife Amy, and my daughters Alina and Elise, whose love, patience and encouragement remind me what is truly important in life.

I would also like to thank my mum and dad, Carol and Ian, for their ongoing love and support, and for the way they raised my brother, Daniel and I in the tradition of storytelling. And thanks to my dad, who proofread every chapter of this book to ensure that it made sense and was worth reading.

Thanks also goes to Daniel for his friendship and love as we grew up and continue to grow together. Not surprisingly, storytelling is a big part of his life, too, and I would like to thank him for his expert advice and guidance as I wrote this book.

I also thank my mother and father-in-law, Lesley and Graham, for all of their love and support that they show our family every day.

I am deeply grateful to Dave Kelly, who was a great friend throughout the process of writing this book and held me accountable every step of the way, checking in with me on a weekly basis to ensure I hit my weekly word count to keep me on target, and then read my drafts to ensure that the chapters made sense and were of value to my audience. Dave, your comments led to some big changes and countless small ones and the book is better thanks to your feedback.

And thank you to Steven Watson who was a constant source of inspiration to me and a great friend throughout this writing process. Out of the blue would come these encouraging messages from someone who had gone before me, and if I wasn't feeling it, I knew I could pick up the phone and he would inspire me to keep going.

Thank you to Alex Gregory-Chialton who proofread and held me accountable in the early stages of my research and writing process. You helped set me up for success.

Thank you to every guest that I've had the pleasure of talking with on our Rule the World Podcast. The generosity with which you have shared knowledge and wisdom has been humbling and has furthered my knowledge and that of our listeners.

Thank you to Andy Gorman for your ongoing friendship, moral support and advice.

Thank you to Andrew Gibson for your never-ending friendship and support, and your introduction to my wonderful publisher Rick Armstrong, who I would also like to thank for your energy, advice and – well – for publishing my book.

And finally, to Rachel Wade, and Zach Greaves, my copywriters, who have done a wonderful job making sure that my Ts are crossed and my Is are dotted – thank you.

Lightning Source UK Ltd.
Milton Keynes UK
UKHW020631120922
408721UK00009B/1076